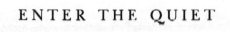

ENTER THE QUIET

... Enter the Quiet

EVERYONE'S WAY TO MEDITATION

JAMES WHITEHILL

HARPER & ROW, PUBLISHERS

SAN FRANCISCO

Cambridge
Hagerstown
Philadelphia
New York

1817

London
Mexico City
Sao Paulo
Sydney

FIRST EDITION

Designed by Jim Mennick

Library of Congress Cataloging in Publication Data

Whitehill, James.
  Enter the quiet.

  Bibliography: p. 170
  1. Meditation.   I. Title.
BL627.W48   1980   158   79-2996
ISBN 0-06-069365-7

80 81 82 83 84 10 9 8 7 6 5 4 3 2 1

Contents

Acknowledgments

This book emerged from courses in meditation I have taught over a period of ten years in the hospitable environment of Stephens College in Columbia, Missouri. Stephens College made possible research in Japan through its faculty research program, granted a sabbatical leave during which the book was written, and provided the teaching freedom necessary for the development of my meditation courses within the Department of Religion and Philosophy. Department colleagues, especially Richard Ray and Richard Gelwick, were personally supportive of the project for several years and helped improve the text by their criticism.

For key insights on the practice of meditation, I am indebted to Masao Abe, who gave his time to me on several occasions in Kyoto in 1975 and 1979. Bill Alexander of Harper & Row, acting as editor, helped me considerably by his suggestions on improving the book and by his understanding of its purposes.

More than 250 Stephens College students of all ages have engaged in the meditation training program, helping to perfect it by their comments and encouraging its wider distribution by their enthusiasm and achievements. They have taught me much about the nature and promise of meditation in everyday American life.

This book is dedicated to my family, who gave me the space and time necessary to meditate and write the book without interference, distraction, or complaint. Pat, Becky, and Ethan understood, and I am grateful for that and for them.

JAMES WHITEHILL

Columbia, Missouri
August 1979

Introduction 02/19/06

Most popular books on meditation vibrate with the excitement of secret spiritual authority. The authors are gurus, masters, or experts with beautifully exotic names: Maharishi Mahesh Yogi, Chögyam Trungpa, Shunryu Suzuki, or even His Divine Grace A. C. Bhaktivedanta Swami Prabhupada. Or the authors may be the American disciples of these Asian sages, writing books while in retreat at the guru's Himalayan village or while sitting at his feet in the quiet of a California valley. The author of *this* book, however, claims no spiritual authority and no descent through an aeons-long line of teachers. While I have visited India and Japan, experienced the special presence of swamis and Zen teachers, and gratefully received the advice and instruction of many in my efforts to learn about and develop the practice of meditation,

I write, think, and feel from the perspective of a professor of religion and philosophy who practices meditation and seeks to make it real and effective within the context of contemporary American life.

This book on meditation is an exploration and invitation to fit meditation to Americans as we live, go about our business, make decisions, and try to cope, work, and love for the best in America. Most books on meditation are fascinating to read, interesting to think about ("Is that *the way* to truth and peace?" "Could I or should I try meditation, become a spiritual athlete, fly to India, enroll in a yoga class, visit a Trappist monastery, or find my guru?"), and largely irrelevant to the interests, situations, and needs of most, if not all, Americans. Reading most of the books, we are left with the impression that meditation is slightly foreign, somewhat obscure—a useful technique of self-improvement or a heroically difficult spiritual lifestyle —but rather removed from the American way of life, vaguely threatening to it, an activity that does not quite fit us or our environment.

Is meditation possible where we are, in American families and communities, in Grand Rapids and Birmingham? Or is it reserved for the few who detach themselves from everyday life, taking up a special way of life in the community of a master who has reached highest, perfect enlightenment? Can we learn and practice meditation without going to India, Japan, or the transplanted Asian meditation center down the street? The truth is that we can learn, practice, and apply basic and advanced meditation exercises and attitudes quite well wherever we are. To explore the practices and discover the very real benefits of meditation, we need only to begin right now, with a minimum of guidance.

The second part of this book, a training program in meditation exercises, provides a progressive learning process that leads from the basics of meditation through more advanced exercises to a completing project in a personal meditation exercise. The exercises are simply described and illustrated, require no elaborate physical postures, and are relevant to daily life. They lead to a flexible, open, and healthy ability to meditate.

However, this is not simply a book on "how to meditate." It also explores the meaning of meditation in America. In the essays of the first part, I urge that we reconsider the shape and purpose of meditation when it is done in America by Americans. The essays describe the American meditation "scene," the process and techniques of meditation, traditional and modern environments for meditation, and its moral and religious dimensions. I believe that the time has come for meditation in America to become American, that is, to become engaged with American realities; to free meditators from dependence on and fascination with exotic, often Asian, sources and teachers; and to bring the insights of meditation to bear upon some ugly and harmful features of American life. Meditation properly practiced and fully understood is a powerful and creative force of moral significance that can and should be put to use in making whole and good the lives of Americans.

The history of meditation reveals that this method of self-changing has been applied to religious purposes in individuals' search for an ultimate and satisfying selfhood; to artistic purposes in relieving tensions and opening the unconscious to inspection; and to selfish purposes in empowering people for the struggle to exist and achieve victory or power over others. Now, however, meditation has come to America, and its primary field of application will not be in religious, artistic, psychological, or selfish activities. Meditation in America will take root, if it does take root, in the soil of our moral concerns for human dignity, justice, and harmony. Toward this goal this book is directed. Learning meditation, we should become energetic, practical, and peaceful; applying meditation to American life, we should become more free, more loving, and more profoundly helpful to ourselves and to others.

Going beyond the noise of self and of America, enter into the quiet of meditation, discovering there a new self, a new America.

.... Part One

REFLECTIONS ON
MEDITATION IN THE
AMERICAN SETTING

CHAPTER 1

The Americanization of Meditation

For more than 200 years, Americans energetically focused on the tasks of building a new nation and a new people. Settling the land, cutting ties with the Old World, creating a new and revolution-born form of government, struggling in violence to establish the unity and meaning of "the American experiment," extending national frontiers, absorbing waves of immigrants, developing the world's largest industrial environment, engaging in several modern wars—American culture was on the move, progressing, boisterous, and optimistic. In the 1960s and 1970s, however, limits to American growth and development were reached, and stubborn problems began to irritate and frustrate the American desire to perfect democracy, to increase unendingly the material standard of living, to preserve freedom and decency, and to discover and conquer new frontiers. The culture of ideals, values, and hopes that fueled the building of a nation seemed now to crack and sigh under the strains of perfecting and consolidating it. America became, in the minds of some, an _Amerika_ that featured big bureaucratic government, a growing tendency to treat people as numbers, corruption in high places and despair in others, moral cynicism, race and class conflict, wars planned by computer and judged by body count, and a degraded natural environment.

Disillusioned in many ways with an America run amuck on the national scale, Americans applied themselves to smaller sources of hope and areas of activity: The nation might go to blazes, but the local community, the family, the job, or even oneself as a separate individual could be worked upon, improved, perfected. These areas were also under stress, however, becoming less secure and reaching the point of breakdown. Local communities were not insulated enough from big government and national organizations to go their own way economically, culturally, or religiously. Nuclear families were not sufficient in size or resources to resist external pressures and offer a refuge from the world. Changes in sexual mores and in the status and aspirations of many women placed further pressure on many families. Too few Americans found their jobs the locus of self-satisfaction, where personal ideals could be found, tested and enjoyed. Those working in the industrial sectors of the economy were subjected to boring routine, trivialized or highly specialized tasks, and growing job insecurity. The growing number of people in the service occupations also were hemmed in by the specialization of their roles, although most service jobs did involve interaction with people more than machines. The fortunate few in the professions of law, teaching, medicine, and ministry were not immune to self-doubt, criticism of the costs and effects of their specialties, and the pressures of conflict and competition in their lives. Small farmers were leaving family farms; business-leaders became more and more subject to government regulation and economic uncertainties. A growing and distressed army of people could not find jobs, so even the self-confidence that comes with having a job, so important to Americans, was unavailable to many.

In reaction, many people tried to create meaning and satisfaction by applying their energies to a last resource—themselves. Throwing themselves into education, tennis, television football, karate, frisbeeing, sports of all sorts, therapy and encounter groups, do-it-yourself activities, travel, and crafts, Americans sought a sense of control over their lives, a refuge from social confusion and moral uncertainty, a feeling of completion and identity. Some Americans, more broken by cultural and social pressures, more disillusioned and alienated, or more adventurous, quested for themselves in drugs that pepped them up, calmed them down, altered their perceptions and feelings, "blew their minds," but, in sum, did little to liberate the people or reconstruct the old culture.

A few Americans, opposing the so-called establishment, deliberately set out to construct a new culture. Collecting in small groups in cities or migrating to mountains and farm, they attempted, with more failure than success, to revitalize themselves by experimenting with communal family forms, traditional crafts, interpersonal relationships, the arts, and their own bodies, minds, and souls. Self-styled new pioneers of the American cultural saga, they variously announced, hoped for, and exhibited a new culture, an alternative or counterculture, based on a new consciousness that would gradually change or "green" America.

The general dissatisfaction of a significant portion of Americans with their cultural values, social institutions, and personal lives made possible the introduction of alternative beliefs and practices into the American mainstream. Many alternative ways of believing, valuing, and acting that were latent within American culture made their appearance, but it often seemed that Americans were turned off by so much of American life that only something from abroad would excite them again. It is no surprise, then, that Asian cultures, so different from our own, suddenly broke in upon us as we searched for credible alternatives. Borrowed entire by new American disciples of Eastern religions, used by artists, interpreted by journalists and intellectuals, Asian cultures became a focus of attention, fascination, and business. Exporting "freedom" and delivering death to Vietnam, Americans were importing gurus, music, martial arts, and meditation from Asia. Ironically, while much of Asia was straining to throw off old cultures in order to enter the modern age of nationalism, technology, and government oriented toward the people, many Americans were seeking the opposite as they moved into an Asian interlude. While young Peace Corps members dug wells for fresh water in Bengal, their brothers and sisters were bathing in the charisma of Hindu swamis in Los Angeles and "digging" His Holiness Maharishi Mahesh Yogi, a former Indian engineering student, in Hollywood.[1]

The high tide of Asian cultural influence in America shows signs of receding, as Americans turn back to the tasks of understanding and reconstructing American society and values. The withdrawal from Vietnam, concern with hard economic and environmental realities, and absorption in Watergate tended to shift our interests away from the radical cultural questioning of the 1960s and early 1970s and from the interest in things Asian. We seem to be readying ourselves for a serious commitment to work on American problems, to face them in such a way that older American values will be clarified and strengthened in the process. Traditional American ideals of self-sacrifice, tolerance, hard work, fairness and reliance on the individual and local community are once again being broadcast and put to use.

The brief opening of America to Asian influence in religion, values, the arts, and sentiment has left its marks, not the least of which are the many religious movements and communities of Asian origin deposited like seeds around America. Hindu ashrams, Tibetan Buddhist meditation centers, Japanese Zen communities, and other religiously inspired places still draw thousands who find in their special environments what they cannot find in themselves and in busy America. Founded and directed by Asians of sincerity and spiritual training, these centers provide Americans, particularly young adults, an alternative and protective environment in which to learn and develop new identities and lifestyles.[2]

The Asian religious communities now in our midst, like the monasteries of historical Christianity and the utopian communities of America, are based on the assumption that the achievement of high religious, cultural, and individual goals requires a period of training in a specially designed and ordered environment separated to some degree from the world of everyday life. To hear God, to learn to love unselfishly, to heal and make ourselves whole, we must retreat temporarily— or for a lifetime—from the noise of business, the competitive struggle for success, and the setting in which we became ill and broken. For most members of the new Asian religious communities, their attachment to and residence in a community is temporary, lasting from a few months to perhaps three years, after which they return to secular life, taking jobs and starting families. Perhaps a few thousand Americans will come to live out their lives within such communities, but even the communities that provide for a full life cycle of membership usually encourage members to interact with the outside world through employment, social service, publishing, or recruiting of new members.

In general, the Asian-oriented communities reveal two differing patterns of religious approach and cultural interaction. On the one hand, several communities and movements are religiously centered in *devotion* to either a divine incarnation (as with the International Society for Krishna Consciousness's dedication to Lord Krishna) or to some tangible person or object which reveals the divine love and power (as with Nichiren Shoshu of America's adoration of the Lotus Sutra scroll or Divine Light Mission's dependence on the grace of the young Guru Maharaji). In this pattern of devotional religion, the focus of religious attention is upon a source of power, love, and authority apparently outside oneself, to which or whom one surrenders one's self and life in humble gratitude, receiving in return an experience of being loved, strengthened, freed, and "reborn." There is an interesting similarity here to the devotional pattern evident in some areas of Christianity, such as the recent charismatic awakening and the so-called Jesus movement. Furthermore, the social outlooks of Christian and Asian devotionally oriented communities both tend to be indifferent to the tasks of social reconstruction and thus appear in a conservative light. The devotional communities usually require a strict standard of personal conduct, involving prohibitions against drug use, sexual activity before and outside marriage, certain foods, and certain profane entertainments. Both to symbolize the initiates' break from the past and to provide a new identity, some of these communities give new names to members and, in the case of the Hare Krishna movement (International Society for Krishna Consciousness), for instance, provide a special haircut, distinctive robes, and a vegetarian diet.

Devotional communities of Asian origin, in their absorption with the activities of worship, attention to details of personal conduct and private moral feeling, and focus on the relationship between the self and the divine, provide a coherent, emotionally rich, and insulated context and lifestyle disengaged from the troubles of the outside world. Many people will be helped personally and uplifted spiritually by the protected structure of dependence and feeling to be found in such groups. But it seems doubtful that they will have much effect upon American culture and its troubles, given their indifference, their weakness in social ethics, and their lack of commitment in facing worldly ambiguities and tensions. Their recipe for American health often seems to be a vague but zealous call to give oneself to Maharaji, praise Krishna, or chant, "Namu myoho renge kyo" ("adoration to the Lotus Sutra").

A contrasting pattern of religious orientation and involvement with American culture can be found in Asia-rooted religious communities like the Integral Yoga Institute of Swami Satchidananda and the various Zen Buddhist organizations derived from Japanese origins. Here we find a religiously understood attempt to discipline and perfect oneself, by one's own powers and will, in order to achieve a state of "natural" and "divine" harmony. By a community regimen of self-inspection, work and exercise, and meditation practices, followers of the religious path of meditation support each other's inward struggle to harmonize body and mind, action and thought, commitment and freedom. The meditation communities provide environments for and training in an almost bewildering variety of meditation methods. Often, the practice, that is, the daily pattern of meditation, work, and group support, becomes an end in itself and issues into a lifestyle characterized by physical health, emotional control, intellectual sharpness, optimism, and calmness. Perhaps influenced by or imitating their Asian teachers, who serve as guides and examples rather than as divine beings, the meditators in these communities appear to have developed a keen sense of humor in the midst of their serious, concentrated lives.

The Asian teachers in these meditation communities seem to varying degrees to resist the attempts of their students to "go Asian," guiding them instead toward an awareness of the values and needs of their present situation in America. Rather than see the meditation community as a retreat from American culture, they view it as the training ground for reentering American society, perhaps for the benefit of America. Zen Center of San Francisco, for example, wisely requires new members to practice meditation for at least a year in the inner-city building before they can retreat to the more vigorous, but also "more Japanese," Tassajara monastery in the Big Sur region of mountains, pines, and mystical mists. Zen Center sees the mountain monastery, the inner-city building, and its Green Gulch farm as complementary environments for spiritual, meditation-focused training and growth. Moving among the three environments, Zen students become environmentally flexible and adaptable, thereby losing or at least weakening the conception that their spiritual growth and practice are special and delicate, to be pursued without contact and engagement with such tasks as cooking, farming, making clothes, cleaning toilets, and in the inner-city building, cooperating with neighbors to resist urban blight and fight city hall.

If meditation communities and spiritual-personal growth centers are to make a significant contribution to the reconstruction of American values and society, they must carefully balance the isolation required for a learning environment with the connection and engagement relevant to the needs of society. Ideally, such communities and centers in America will be more than refuges for retreating Americans. They will be places that heal but also places that experiment, teach, and apply the values, attitudes, practices, and specific skills needed in the everyday world by everyday people. We have a right to expect that such places will give us people, ideas, practical sciences, and models that will show or point the way to the good conduct of our life in America. If, as they all claim, the truth and goodness we seek are beyond the Asian trappings in which they come to us, then we have a right to expect these communities to wean themselves of their attachment to and dependency on Asian surfaces—clothing, diets, architecture, and teachers. We expect them, in other words, to go through a process of Americanization.

A critical stumbling block to Americanization in most well-organized religious communities of Asian origin is one source of their vitality: the Asian-born and Asian-cultured leader. Initially, these leaders *by their difference,* as expressed in speech, clothing, and general demeanor, will attract Americans to their sides with the promise of a new way. But eventually the issues must be faced as to whether to dress like the leader, study his language, look to his homeland as Mecca, and replace him with someone like him from Asia when he retires or dies—or not. Communities that remain attached to the superficial aspects of their Asian origins will almost certainly fail to make a significant, long-term contribution to the reconstruction of America. Before his death in 1971, the Japanese founder of the San Francisco Zen Center appointed an American, Richard Baker, as his spiritual and organizational successor, emphasizing by the choice both his confidence in Baker and his desire that Zen students see their spiritual growth as a process basically free of Japanese roots, since the enlightened self was at home and with roots everywhere. As Asian founders of the new religious communities retire and die in the coming years, we must expect some of their followers to fail in this critical test of Americanizing their leadership and, thereby, its influence upon and assistance to mainstream America. Rather, they will import new leaders from Asia who, like the Christian missionaries of not long ago, are unable to or refuse to adapt to the new setting, limiting their understanding and helpfulness in America.

If the Asian leader is the center of emotional and organizational vitality in these religious communities, Asian meditation techniques are often the central method by which members of the communities achieve their goals of disciplining and perfecting themselves. Viewed in one way, the effect of the community leader and the purpose of the special environment of the religious community are to support, inspire, and protect the process of meditation, the program of changing the self through more or less vigorous exercises of physical, emotional, intellectual, and spiritual dimensions. The practice of these exercises, under the guidance of a teacher in a special, controlled environment, is the essence of the religious path in the view of some religious communities. While the meditation can be viewed as a means to the end of becoming a better person, there is a general tendency, in line with Asian tradition, to view meditation as an end in itself. Pursued for its own sake, meditation is not viewed narrowly: It is a way of life, a basic orientation toward oneself, others, the world, and God. In this view, doing meditation is not merely doing physical and mental exercises to achieve some goals which are *beyond* meditation. Doing meditation is, rather, the practice and expression of an orientation and an attitude in all activities, whether it is washing the dishes, singing, walking in the woods, weeding the garden, or building a new society. All of life, even dying, becomes a context of meditation. Indeed, from this point of view life at its best *is* meditation—the calm, energetic and resourceful reconciliation of oneself with the world, with oneself, with God.

When separated from the view that they are the method of a total meditative lifestyle, meditation exercises tend to become a technique or skill system cut loose from the moral and spiritual goals of religious communities. Since the beginning stages of meditation result in specific psychological and physical benefits, it is possible and not uncommon to find meditation promoted as a means to physical fitness, as in the many physical yoga schools, as a substitute for the so-called highs of drug experience, as a reliever of tension and stress, or as a means to psychological health. It is rare to find meditation promoted in these terms within the religous communities.

Not only do they see meditation as clearly linked with moral and spiritual goals, they are also keenly aware that as meditators progress deeper into meditation, problems of high stress, psychological disorder, and physical illness may arise.

Nowadays, however, most Americans are exposed to meditation by those who view it as a technique, a secular, quasi-psychological tool for achieving psychological or other goals divorced from moral awareness and spiritual direction. The secularization of meditation is advanced by journalists, psychologists, and some Asian meditation teachers, in part because they are speaking to what they believe is a culture nonreligious in orientation.

The separation of meditation exercises from a clear moral and religious context is no more interestingly apparent than in Transcendental Meditation, the simplified and popular form of meditation first taught in this country by Maharishi Mahesh Yogi and later by thousands of his American students. Apparently a student of a Hindu guru, the Maharishi ("Great Teacher") left the Himalayas after thirteen years of meditation with specific instructions to regenerate and pacify the world with the Transcendental Meditation message. Deciding that the United States was a fertile field in which to sow the TM teaching, he made his way to this country in the 1960s, attracting young celebrities as students and appearing on the Johnny Carson *Tonight* Show. At first, his appearance in monk's robes and long beard, and with flowers in hand, suggested that he was another Hindu guru come to tell us of the peace to be had through yoga, vegetarianism, the life of poverty, and union with the universal spirit. Appearances were deceiving.[3]

The Maharishi and his followers stressed from the beginning that Transcendental Meditation was not a religion, but a technique; that it was not limited by its cultural origin in India, but was universal and natural; that it need not be practiced in a committed community, but was a matter of private individual practice; that no prior moral examination and development were necessary to its practice, for anyone had an equal opportunity to take up the technique; and, finally, that TM was compatible with modern science. The single stress upon the technique and its personal benefits and the denial of the traditional trappings of meditation resulted in a simplified, non-threatening, individual-centered, and secular appeal for TM. Hundreds of thousands of Americans have found the Maharishi's description sufficiently inviting to enroll in TM courses, receive their mantra, and call themselves meditators.

The accomplishment of the Maharishi and the TM movement, in the context of the Americanization of meditation, should not be dismissed, underestimated, or misunderstood. More than anyone else, the Maharishi has succeeded in removing both the appeal and the threat of the exotic that are often attached to meditation. Both in his interpretation and in the TM meditation technique, the Maharishi has assured Americans that basic meditation is simple, natural, and healthy, and he has enabled many Americans to begin meditation. Presenting meditation as a scientific technique for the development of our "Creative Intelligence," he has cast meditation in terms with which we are mostly comfortable, tied it into the values Americans see in science and creativity and freed it from organized religion to the extent that some public schools and even the armed forces are possibly considering teaching TM with public money. Linking the practice of TM with the everyday concerns of Americans, the Maharishi provides us with the technique and assurance by which we can learn to relax more deeply away from tension; to restore our energies; and, hence, to pursue our immediate goals of working more efficiently, studying with greater intensity, becoming less nervous, and enjoying life. Not always sure of what the happiness we pursue is or how to achieve it, some Americans now find it in twice-a-day TM practice, as their minds "naturally move to deeper and deeper levels of happiness within" (to quote TM's self-description). The happiness we seek is within us, says the Maharishi and his student-teachers, and TM is the easiest and surest technique for reaching it.

While Transcendental Meditation has adapted its message and technique increasingly to the American context, largely by denying its religiousness and affirming its "scientific" validity, it probably will be of little usefulness or influence in meeting the social, cultural, and moral needs of America. By reducing a way of life to a technique, by shedding its religious origins in favor of a naive faith in science, by abandoning clear concepts of community in order to focus on individuals, by avoiding any demand upon the conscience of individuals (except that they pay the moderate fees for instruction), and by misleading people about the nature and potential of meditation, TM has adjusted too well and, perhaps, abandoned too much. We may now wonder what is "transcendental" in Transcendental Meditation except that we can transcend or go beyond a troubled self and society into "levels of happiness." Americans and America need healing; TM may be only an aspirin, masking the symptoms and dulling the pains.

Transcendental Meditation, which has and will accomplish much in helping thousands of people to bring themselves into a state of mind and body more healthy than they knew before, fails us in the long run in our responsibility to work and care for others and for the reconstruction of values in America. The likely source of TM's failure is in the Maharishi's repeated and misleading insistence that meditation is natural and easy. This description of meditation is important and very useful in the context of beginning meditation, where beginners must be free of anxiety, stress, and other pressures about meditation itself in order to meditate. Even after the beginner has caught the drift of how the meditation process flows, if thoughts arise that we are really accomplishing something, that "I" am *willing* myself into the state—in other words, that TM is not natural or spontaneous—the result is interruption of the meditation. So a wise meditation teacher always says, "Don't worry about meditation. Just do the practice and all will come about spontaneously and naturally if you don't interfere by thinking about it." By stressing the naturalness and ease of meditating, the teacher is both recommending an attitude of relaxation and warning against the disturbing thought that "I am responsible for this state, *I* am the one doing it, *I* did it!" If the thought arises during meditation, "I am doing it," meditation ceases with that self-consciousness. The interruption and its consequences can be compared to the situation where we 'naturally" and "spontaneously" wad a piece of paper and throw it successfully into the wastebasket several feet away. Surprised at our skill, we may try to do it again, deliberately—only to fail.

Much of the uneasiness many thoughtful people have about Maharishi's naivete or indifference toward moral questions and issues of social justice results from his notions (derived probably from the fact that he is primarily a teacher of a technique and not a moralist or a Buddha) that you cannot do anything in meditation if you think *you* can do it. You do meditation by letting go of the idea that *you* do meditation. When asked about poverty, war, and suffering, the Maharishi offers no sophisticated analysis or urgent cry for peace and justice. He simply says that by easily and naturally meditating, people will become moral, and the world made up of or influenced by such meditators will be in harmony. Concerned citizens regard such a vague answer as naive at best. Some say he has little feeling for moral agony and has not experienced evil. Perhaps, but, as a meditation teacher, he is probably correct to insist that we not allow ourselves to tighten up and become self-conscious and self-righteous as a way to fight evil.[4] We are probably better off and more successful, much of the time, if we resist injustice, struggle against suffering, and ward off evil with the attitude that to do so is the natural and easy thing to do or that it is the Holy Spirit working through us that is doing the work. TM people are now saying that if one percent of the world's, or a community's, population practiced TM, crime and drug abuse would decrease, injustice would diminish, the economy would improve, and peace would be achieved. Easily. Naturally.

This is foolish talk to the moralists among us, who prefer to see goodness as the fruit of heroic struggle and sacrifice. After his wife began TM, Kurt Vonnegut, Jr., wrote that he held the following conversation with her:

> "What kind of a holy man is it that talks economics like a traveling secretary of the National Association of Manufacturers?"
>
> "People *make* him talk economics. He doesn't want to talk about them. They aren't his field," she says.
>
> "How come he bombed in India, the home of meditators, and then had great success with middle-class people in Scandinavia and West Germany and Great Britain and America?"
>
> "For many complicated reasons, no doubt."
>
> "Maybe it's because he talks economics like a traveling secretary of the National Association of Manufacturers."
>
> "Think what you like," she says, loving me, loving me, loving me. She smiles.
>
> "If this thing is so good," I say, "Why doesn't Maharishi take it right into the slums, where people are really suffering?"
>
> "Because he wants to spread the word as fast as possible, and the best way to do that is to start with influential people."
>
> "Like The Beatles."
>
> "Among others."
>
> "I can see where influential people would like Maharishi better than Jesus. My God, if The Beatles and Mia Farrow went to Jesus, He'd tell 'em to give all their money away."
>
> And my wife smiles.[5]

To people like Vonnegut, smiling and relaxing, radiating happiness and contentment are neither moral goods nor ways to the good. The pursuit of goodness, thirsting for truth and justice, and righting the world's wrongs seem to require pain, struggle, tension, and an aggressive spirit. The Maharishi suggests that if we allow ourselves to easily and naturally meditate, we will discover and express easily our natural goodness. Neither view, of course, is entirely satisfactory. Vonnegut should remember that the quest for goodness and justice must be accompanied by a sense of final harmony and should see fruit in the grace, pleasure, and beauty of good acts and good people. The Maharishi apparently has not learned that most people, in pursuing justice and righteousness, must struggle deeply and long with themselves and with "principalities and powers." In the ordinary sense of the words, it is not obviously easy or natural to seek, do, or be good. To be and do good requires blood, sweat, tears, and the help of others, and a keen sense of original sin, of our "natural" tendency to seek our own selfish interest.

Meditation is a valuable practice for many, a possible lifestyle for some, so long as the process of meditation is turned to moral concerns and assists us to be better to and with each other, recognizing the difficulties of doing the good. The difficulty of knowing and doing the good is recognized most clearly in the Western traditions of Judaism and Christianity, to which most Americans are heirs. The practice of meditation that remains locked up in a Buddhist temple in Los Angeles, in a special community gathered around an Asian leader in Minneapolis, or in the isolated individualism of a TMer is, finally, irrelevant to America. The Americanization of meditation means that meditation practice will gradually be shaped to fit what America is and what America ought to be. While we are not at the point where we can see clearly and fully what American meditation will and should be, we can at least now see what it cannot and should not be. It cannot be dependent on or a reflection of Asian sources, leaders, and cultural values, valuable and useful though they be. It should not be a tool confined to individualistic needs and narrowed by a secular, vague morality.

The Americanization of meditation means that the exercises and technique must be deepened beyond what TM offers, so that meditation becomes a practice of everyday life, enriching and enriched by our shared and most lofty moral concerns and values. The Americanization process also demands attention to the environments which both hinder and help the practice of meditation. Environments that are suitable for meditation at its wholesome best are also environments that are healthy for all people, including the broken, the poor in spirit, the disillusioned, and the pained. In seeking such environments, we are looking for a place in which the Kingdom of God within can be found. But in building such environments, we are working toward the City of God on earth and expressing a commitment to our brothers and sisters. The Americanization of meditation will be achieved when it is no longer necessary to go to a special place insulated from American reality to take up the practice and all it can mean. That future achievement depends on putting meditation to work in, for, and by Americans in the troubled American setting.

How does TM answer the need in America? It doesn't answer the need of the poor.

The Practice

Most Americans take one of two views on what the practice of meditation means in terms of goals, commitments of energy, technical difficulties, and setting. On the one hand, we can see meditation activities as doing something that Transcendental Meditation students do. To achieve their goals of becoming more calm or less nervous or more energetic or more "happy," TMers commit themselves to a seven-hour training program stretching over a week. During the training program, they fill out a questionnaire, hear lectures on Transcendental Meditation, interview *How!* with their teachers for no more than an hour, receive a *mantra* or syllable-sound formula for use as a mental focus during meditation, and then are checked after a week or so of practicing the technique. The practice, or program and process of meditation, involves meditation no more than twice per day *Time* for twenty-minute periods each time. TM requires virtually no moral preparation or screening before newcomers are taught the technique, nor does it require physical conditioning or the *Not!* learning of difficult body postures. Reducing meditation to the basic and beginning techniques of all meditation systems, TM by its simplicity allows anyone and everyone to take up the practice, with a minimum of rearrangement of life and an immediate result in decreased tension, increased feelings of well-being, and increased energy for most tasks. Meditation, in this picture, is easy and simple, pleasurable and useful.

The other picture Americans have of meditation is very different. In the classical forms of Christian and other religious traditions, the goals of meditation seem lofty, the commitment total, the practice complex, the difficulties many and subtle. Whether we have in mind the lifelong progress through states of consciousness of the Hindu yogi, the prolonged struggle of the soul to rise beyond itself to God in Christian saints, or the highly disciplined, almost military life of the Zen Buddhist monk, in this view we tend to see meditation as a difficult and long process which only spiritual athletes can undergo. Classical meditation is a far-reaching contest against our habitual self in order to reach and unite with the heart and mind of "Reality." This is the meditation of the mystics, the special few who, abandoning the world, seek Something or Someone beyond the noise and confusion of ordinary life. Living in prayer cells, caves, or protected monasteries, practicing a lifestyle of poverty and chastity, and engaged in long hours of meditation each day, year after year, the classical meditators elicit our awe and respect.

These two popular views of meditation are difficult to

reconcile and also misleading if we are to understand the nature and potential of meditation in the American setting. Both views are extremes that neglect the truth about meditation contained in the opposing view. Meditation is easy and yet there are difficulties; almost anyone can learn the beginnings of meditation, but it takes a moral act of will to press beyond the beginnings; meditation can be practiced in almost all situations and environments, but practicing meditation in any depth requires a particularly suited environment. If we seek a practical meditation for Americans, one that will be of real help in meeting the demands our culture places upon moral and responsive people, we must take a middle path between the extreme views. We need a practice that is not so simple that it ignores us as moral and spiritual beings who ought to take action to change ourselves and America for the better. We need a form of meditation practice that we can do, but one which challenges and works us, links us to the nature and destiny of America, helps us join with others at the same time that it helps us help ourselves. Finally, we need a meditation practice that helps set us free and frees others. The moral touchstones of a mature meditation are freedom, courage, and compassion, and an American meditation must bear fruit in these virtues so much needed today.

The Basics of Meditation: Practicing the Three B's

What, exactly, do people do when they meditate? How does meditation work? Fundamentally, meditation is the practice of changing a habitual attitude or orientation to the world. Ordinarily, we learn, through the influences of family, friends, and society, habits of body posture, emotion, thought, and judgment in order to adjust to the expectations of others. From these learned habits we build up a set or pattern of physical and mental behavior that helps us "get along," "behave ourselves," "cope," "fit in," and "become a success," in terms of a group or social situation. Through the practice of these habits we gain a sense of belonging and security, as well as a role and identity, that are somewhat clear and consistent. If asked, "Who are you?" I can point to my being male, a college teacher, a family man, and so on. Beyond these general roles, however, I can point to other habits which pin down further who I am: I am the person who likes to sleep late, who watches Sunday football games, prefers beer to wine, does not like to wear a suit, and putters around the house and yard. I have other habits, too, by which you and I can recognize "me." I like to think a lot before acting or deciding, but not before speaking. I become angry when the newspaper arrives late, when I do not finish my work on time, when my clothes do not fit, and when I cannot remember something. I enjoy this or that. I love my family, my friends, my fishing pole, my country. Indeed, I am a pattern of habitual attachments, likes and dislikes, predictable responses. But "I" am also more than these habits, for I can become aware of them and change them.

Meditation, at its simplest, is a group of activities by which we develop a new set of habits to counter our ordinary physical, emotional, and mental habits. The meditator learns, practices, and masters a set of physical postures, emotional responses, and mental attitudes that are in contrast to his learned, socially useful, and routine habits. By practicing the meditation set of habits each day, the meditator is gradually freed from his habitual self as the only and dominating experience of himself, and from his habitual world as the only and dominating environment for him. This freeing up comes from a change in attitude, the basic, unconscious way in which we sense our self (Am "I" usually found in my head?), perceive things (Is my car a "big metal thing" or is it my "home away from home?"), respond to people (Are they trying to use me? Where did she get that dress?), and interpret the world (Is it confusing, threatening, to be conquered, headed for destruction, or "my oyster"?). The meditator temporarily drops all these habits by experimentally taking up an attitude that poses a different experience of self, of others and things, and of the world. This meditative attitude is like opening up a new vista, like becoming a child again, like cleaning the doors of perception, or like moving from bondage to freedom (in a fresher, more open view). While some see the view or attitude achieved in meditation as the real and true view and the old attitude as one of ignorance, illusion, or sinfulness, it is more likely that meditation simply provides an alternative, different, newer view on the things we have become accustomed to dealing with. The excitement of beginning meditation lies in the freshness and novelty of seeing things differently and not being tied up in the old routines and habits. Doing meditation is, in effect, taking a temporary vacation, vacating the "house" we usually live in, emptying our minds of the usual, automatic responses.

In order to vacate the premises of our habitual views and responses, in order to move to a "new location," in order to change significantly our underlying attitude, we must change our habits of body, emotion, and mind by learning new patterns. Meditation systems focus, to varying degrees, on *body posture, breathing,* and *brain activity,* the three B's. Modification in these three aspects of our self necessarily results in the new perspective on self and life that is the goal of meditation.

Different teachers and systems of meditation will recommend different exercises of body, breathing, and brain. Usually, the more lofty and difficult the goal, the more prolonged and difficult are the techniques; the more prosaic and practical the goal, the more brief and simple the exercises. This distinction is fundamental: we get out what we put in. Beyond that distinction, there are a bewildering and fascinating variety of meditation techniques, exercises, and approaches.[1] Nevertheless, it is quite possible, and certainly desirable, to describe the fundamentals of any meditation in terms of body, breathing, and brain exercises, and to recommend a sensible program to

Americans which is of the proper degree of difficulty, simplicity, and depth.

The initial aim of all meditation techniques is to produce a total state of "relaxed awareness." By alterations of body and mind states, the meditator achieves physical and mental release from stress. This relaxation forms the basis for the gradual development of increased awareness and alertness. The term *relaxed awareness* may seem paradoxical to us. Usually when we conceive of being alert or aware, we imagine someone with eyes wide open, straining to see, sitting on the edge of the seat, every muscle poised for reaction or action. Alert situations are normally seen as situations where we must fight or flee, where fear is high, tension is flying through our muscles, and our minds are racing. But the relaxed awareness that is the basis or starting point of meditation is more like the relaxed and alert state we know in such situations as drifting into or out of sleep, performing a sport effortlessly and gracefully, becoming aware of a sunset in its brilliant presence, or finishing a hard task and basking in self-contentment.

Meditation exercises are designed to relax body and mind, to quiet them, so that we may become aware once the fidgeting of body and chatter of mind have ceased. Once this state is known and can be produced at will, usually after a week or two of daily practice, we can extend and apply it to a variety of situations and needs: meditation for deep relaxation at the office, meditation for quickness and energy in sports, meditation for calmness and balance in conflict encounters, meditation for openness and loving ourselves, friends, and enemies, and so on to other goals and virtues in many settings. Through practice the meditator is able to take up the meditation attitude of relaxed awareness by self-command to achieve goals that tend, over time, to be less selfish, less motivated by fear or greed, and more harmonious with physical, emotional, and mental needs.

The First B: Body Posture as the Root of Meditation

A successful meditation practice is based on an awareness of how our body positions both produce and express emotional and mental states. If we want to produce a relaxed state of mind, we know it helps to sit or lie down. If we want to express an attitude of "I'm relaxed" to ourselves or others, we often adopt a sitting or reclining position. On a less conscious level, if we become relaxed, our muscles tend to loosen, whereas if we are becoming tense in mind, our muscles also tend to become tense. This mutual interaction of body and mind states goes on all the time and becomes clear to others and to ourselves if we just notice the ways in which bodies mirror mind states (as in a smile, hunched shoulders, or hands waving while we talk) and minds mirror body states (as in the incoherence of someone with a fever or the difference in talking while we are standing up or sprawling on the floor.) We can also become aware of the conflicts between mind and body states in situations where the body says one thing and the mind says the opposite. We may say "I'm glad to be here" with our speech, but our rigid body and arms folded tightly say something else. We are "out of synch."

Meditation begins with an awareness of the need to find and sustain a body position appropriate to the state of relaxed awareness. Generally, the proper position is a sitting position, and most meditation practice is done while sitting. While the total state of relaxed awareness can be achieved while lying down, standing, or even running, the easiest position is with the body sitting stably, in an erect manner without stiffness. The sitting position is halfway between the relaxed position of sleep (lying down) and the alert position of action (standing up).

Meditation periods stretch from fifteen minutes to several hours in the case of very advanced meditators. In order to maintain the body in a stable, erect, and relaxed position for this length of time, without slouching, fidgeting, tilting, or stress, meditators have evolved a rather standard set of tricks. The simplest method is to sit in a lightly padded chair with a more or less straight back (like a kitchen chair), placing the feet flat on the floor and folding the hands in the lap. There is a slight slouch or sway in the back which must be eliminated by leaning forward and drawing the back away from the chair. To accomplish this it is necessary to allow your stomach to relax and drop forward and down, which you can only do comfortably if you are not corseted around the waist by a belt or tightly fitting clothes. (This is one reason meditators traditionally wear loose-fitting robes.) In this flat-footed, stomach extended position, the next trick is to drop and relax the shoulders. American men in particular have the habit of lifting and squaring their shoulders; they must let the shoulders drop into a naturally relaxed position. A last check to make sure your body is both relaxed and alert in all areas—especially stomach, shoulders, neck, face, and spine—and you are ready. Your body is already "meditating."

A more stable and traditional sitting position, and one easier to adapt to if you do not live in a "chair-sitting" culture, is the lotus posture known to us through Asian meditation. For Americans, it is usually best to work into the lotus posture by trying the half-lotus posture, sitting on the floor in such a way that the knees, in a cross-legged arrangement, will touch the floor. With one foot tucked in toward the crotch area, the other foot is placed by hand on the other thigh or in the notch between thigh and calf. This is not a fully stable position, but after your muscles become accustomed to this stretched position, you may attempt the full lotus position. In the full lotus both feet are placed on the opposite thighs, the trunk and spine are elevated slightly by a cushion, and the knees touch the floor. A three-point base is thus achieved and can be sustained for hours. Some meditators can even sleep in this posture.

Beginning meditators should probably start by sitting in a chair and progress as soon as they are comfortable with meditation to the half-lotus. These two positions are adequate for the length of time needed in beginning meditation, which is fifteen to thirty minutes in one position, once or twice a day. Meditation changes in quality and difficulty when it is done for more than thirty minutes at a time. For longer periods of meditation, the lotus posture is essential for body stability, and a master of meditation is probably necessary for psychological and spiritual stability because prolonged meditation opens meditators to the deeper levels of unconscious life.

To deepen the relaxation achieved by quieting and "fixing" body posture, meditators should close their eyes when assuming the sitting position. When the eyes are closed, it is useful to throw them out of gear a bit by lightly "looking" at the tip of the nose or the forehead. Our visual habits, expressed in eye postures, must be checked and counteracted if we are to relax sufficiently in meditation. Perhaps closing our eyes also triggers a sleep signal, which further relaxes us—unless we go too far and actually fall asleep, whereupon meditation, which is relaxed awareness or awareness in the state of relaxation, would cease.

To insure a relaxed body posture, the meditator usually wears loose-fitting clothing suitable for the temperature and humidity. If the meditator is too cold or too hot, meditation becomes difficult. Also, relaxation is difficult on a full and digesting stomach, so it is usually necessary to wait at least an hour after eating before going into a meditation period and posture. Other obstacles to a stable, quiet, and relaxed body, such as illness, cramps, muscle tensions, or coughing can be dealt with by modifying one's posture; by ignoring them; or by warming-up exercises, such as walking, calisthenics, or stretching exercises, before sitting down. Sometimes back tensions are so severe that you can only meditate while lying on your back. As long as you do not become drowsy or fall asleep in that position, it is possible for meditation. Simply lie on your back on a rug, allow each part of your body to relax (especially the arch in the small of the back), and begin meditating.

A body posture which is both relaxed and alert is the root or base of meditation. When you sit, you are rooting your body to the ground, planting yourself in preparation for growing into meditation. Imagining that your body is a tree or a half-buried rock, with a right to sit and do nothing but breathe and meditate, is both a help in getting a feel for meditating and a concept with interesting implications in our human-centered, restless, go-getter culture.

The Second B: Breathing as the Flow of Meditation

We all know, but rarely pay direct attention to the fact, that breathing may signify and accompany changes in attitude. The sigh, gasp, or pant, and fast, slow, deep, or shallow breathing all may be seen as reflecting a state of mind in response to an outer situation or inner signal. But we rarely notice these variations, much less attempt to control and alter them. Meditators, however, are almost always noticing, adjusting, or in extreme cases of yoga, manipulating the breathing process. Breathing is seen, and can be experienced, as the important link between body and mind. Once brought under attention and some control, the flow and cycle of breathing become important indicators of and aids to meditation.

Meditative breathing takes many shapes and is subject to a variety of interpretations as to its meaning and importance. Some forms of yoga view breath as the flow of subtle life and energy through the body and psychic centers, and the manipulation of this life force becomes the aim of some exotic exercises, such as holding the breath for long periods or mastering the ability to inhale through one nostril and exhale out the other. Generally, however, meditative breathing consists of a "natural" breathing that is encouraged by self-suggestion and by the body's relaxation to become slower, deeper, and more regular than normal breathing. Meditative breathing resembles breathing during sleep, including occasional spurts and catch-ups of quick breathing.

Beginning meditators, after becoming settled in the sitting position, should gently observe their breathing, noting whether it is fast or slow or irregular. Quietly observing your breath, and not trying to control it, you see that it usually slows down and becomes audible. You can also observe that, when really relaxed, you breath by having your stomach muscles go in and out rather than by having your chest lift and fill. Swelling up the chest and sucking in the stomach, though important to some people, is of no use in meditation. Properly seated, with the stomach free to drop forward and down, with some slight pressure on the stomach muscles during inhalation, the meditator naturally begins deep and regular breathing. This breathing has a calming and relaxing effect on the body, but especially on the mind. Indeed, in the most hectic of environments, paying attention to the regular rise and fall of breathing, the rhythmic pressure on the stomach wall, and the slight sound of exhaling can create a quiet center in the storm.

A further benefit to paying attention to our stomach muscle sensations as we breath in and out is that it locates our attention in the area of our physical center of gravity. So useful or significant is this shift in attention that several meditation traditions assert that our psychic, or soul, center is located in the lower stomach region—two knuckles-width below our belly buttons, in fact. The cliché about navel-gazing thus has its origin in this meditative practice of "feeling" our center in the region just below the navel. Proper meditation breathing, in fact, can be checked by observing whether the stomach muscles below the navel are being extended almost as much as the muscles above the navel. Another benefit to focusing on this region lies in the fact that, to the degree we focus on stomachs we focus less on our facial muscles, on the senses of the head, and on the head. To focus on the head, to locate our habitual self in the head, to think that we think and live through our heads, almost in separation of our heads from our bodies, is to be "top-heavy." By breaking this head-habit, meditators discover that they can call upon more resources of energy of *Head* the whole body, avoid headaches, maintain physical and mental balance more readily, and advance their meditation both in sitting and while engaging in other activities. A meditation master once summed up thus: "When meditating, put your mind in the palm of your left hand (folded in the lap, it rests against the lower stomach wall)."

If meditation is to become practical, something that is extended into everyday activities, meditators must develop the habit of checking breathing and locating attention in the *center*, or region just below the navel. By checking breathing, we know in a second or two whether we are subconsciously agitated or calm, and by centering, we gain in a few seconds a balance of body and mind as well as a securely based and open awareness. Meditation manuals and teachers, unfortunately, do not stress this physical sensation and mental act of centering enough. Without it, there can be little successful or morally generous meditation.

The Third B: Brain Activity as the Flower of Meditation

With the body sitting in a stable, alert, relaxed, and dignified posture and with the breath flowing easily and spontaneously to and from the stomach or center, the meditator has checked and brought under control, to a useful degree, her physical and emotional nature. The control and calm of body and breath gradually allow for mental control, calm, and the special awareness called meditation. Meditators know from experience that harmony of body, breath, and brain is necessary to successful meditation. Tension in one will express itself in the other two, but calmness in one will tend to produce calmness in the other two, so that by the regulation of body, breath, or brain activity, the other two aspects are also brought under a useful degree of control.

Meditators believe that the mind or brain is the most difficult dimension of human nature to change or control. The mind, including subconscious impulses and responses, seems to be like a stream of thought, rushing on and on, bubbling against the rocks of reality, cutting its favorite channels or habits, and surging downward in undertows that are powerful but invisible. The mind is doing many things in every moment, although we may be paying attention to only one thing in each instant. The mind may also be compared to a monkey, restlessly jumping from limb to limb, holding a branch with one arm, a fruit with another, reaching for another branch with a foot, and scratching with the other foot, while the tail is curled around still another branch of another tree. The monkey-mind does several things at once, is always jumping around and grasping things. It cannot put all its energy and awareness into one thing or act, and it cannot relax. The monkey-mind cannot sit still and be quiet.

Beginning meditators, once they have taken up a sitting position and calmed their breathing, become vividly aware of the restless, moving, wandering, and disorderly nature of the mind process. All kinds of thoughts, words, emotions, and perceptions are coursing through awareness, with little connection from one second or minute to the next. The process seems to go on by itself, almost automatically. If the meditator simply *observes* the internal mental process, without becoming interested in it or attached to it, its independent, automatic qualities become quite clear. At the same time it becomes clear that there is a difference between the *thought-process being observed* and *the awareness that is observing*. This difference between thought and awareness leads to the notion that *our self or the place of awareness is different or separate from our thoughts,* our habitual and learned responses to and processing of reality.

Meditation, therefore, is a matter not of thinking, but of deepening and strengthening the experience of being aware. To cultivate awareness, meditators must find techniques to deal with the chatter of thought in the mind, the "noise" that obscures pure awareness and, hence, the self. This pure awareness, issuing from the place of self, has nothing to do with my awareness, just as the self experienced in meditation has little to do with my personality. The awareness and the self are experienced as rather impersonal, as a force, power, or center that seems to exist behind or underneath our usual sense of ourself as thinker and doer. This awareness might be compared to a low hum in our being, and our personality, thoughts, emotions, and movements are like a rapidly changing melody on top of this hum of one note. When the melody pauses, becomes soft, or stops, we become aware of the hum (or the hum becomes aware of itself). Meditation techniques directed at brain activity all have the purpose of making us aware of the hum of awareness by means of quieting the melody, calming the monkey-mind, or stopping the waves of thought.

Two techniques, concentrating on a mental focus and detachment, are used to enhance the meditator's awareness and to diminish the surface chatter of the thought process. The most often used device is a mental focus of some kind to which the meditator attaches his attention. Attempting to concentrate the mind by fixing the attention to one point, one word, one phrase, or one image, the meditator accomplishes, to varying degress, a blocking or suppression of ordinary thought movement, an increased intensity of awareness, a stability and relaxation of mind, and, finally, a stage of nothought, where even the single focus disappears and leaves the meditator in "pure" awareness.

The mental focus used differs from tradition to tradition and person to person. Often the focus is a holy word, like *OM* in Hindu meditation or *God* in Christian meditation. Sometimes the focus is a phrase, like *Lord, our God, have Mercy*, repeated again and again to the exclusion of other thoughts. After a number of repetitions, a word or phrase becomes automatic, or learned, and will carry on by itself. While some verbal foci may be loaded with religious meaning, others seem to work as well in beginning meditation without any meaning. For example, many meditation teachers simply suggest that the beginning meditator focus on counting breaths—*one* on inhalation, *two* on exhalation, *three* on the next inhalation, and so on, up to *ten*, when the counting begins again at *one*. (If we did not remain aware enough to return to *one*, we would continue counting until we lost awareness and fell asleep!) A similar use of a word focus without meaning is evident in TM, where meditators are given a Sanskrit mantra or word-phrase to meditate on, although its original religious meaning is not explained and is viewed as unimportant to the meditation process. The calming effect of focusing on and repeating a word or word sequence is known to all of us who have counted to ten when we were angry. Such a practice interrupts the habitual or learned thought process, detaches the mind from what has started, and brings a mastery over our habitual responses.

Generally, a beginning meditator is best served by using a simple and neutral word or word-sequence as a mental focus or sticking point. Counting up to ten on the inhalations and exhalations is a good example. Using the neutral numbers as foci, the mind is not triggered into a thought process involving past experiences or emotions. Furthermore, by connecting the counting, which is done silently, with the breathing cycle, and by counting from the "center," as if a voice in the navel is doing the counting, the meditator can reinforce the concentration and relaxation of body and mind. A purely mental focus, unconnected to the body or breathing cycle, tends to induce drowsiness or boredom. Counting to ten eventually becomes boring, whereupon more significant words, carrying attitudes, desires, and needs, may be used. The criterion is that the meditator maintain a stable, relaxed, and alert attitude, whatever the mental focus.

Highly developed meditation traditions discovered and experimented with very elaborate mental foci for meditation. Tibetan Buddhist monks are said to construct a mental image, piece by piece, of a religious diagram, or mandala, and to hold all the parts together for hours of meditation, during which they become absorbed into the mandala. The repetition of Jesus's name for hours in meditative quiet and fullness of heart is a Christian practice still found in the Eastern Orthodox church. Buddhist monks in Burma may practice an exercise in which they concentrate on the gentler feelings of love—good will, pity, and sympathy—trying to radiate these feelings continuously around them. Common to these practices is their base in a meditation attitude as well as the belief that if we concentrate on something with all our energy, we become it—we become what we meditate on.

A mental focus, whether simple or elaborate, is in the end a tool of meditation. A fully matured process of awareness therapy or training will finally dispense with the view that to meditate is to concentrate on something to the exclusion of all other things. One must not get trapped in or unconsciously habituated to a specific mental focus, be it counting to ten or reciting the name of God, Buddha, or OM. So most advanced meditation reaches a point where even the mental focus is put aside or it simply disappears in a "cloud of unknowing" or in the "disappearance of the one point." When the mental focus drops away, there is no longer a separation between the awareness of the meditator and the focus of awareness. The meditator becomes identified with the focus ("I am OM"), or both drop away ("I am nothing"), or self and world return to a miraculous simplicity (" I am sitting—I am the sitting").

This last stage, of dropping the technique of mental focusing, is an illustration of the second major technique used in meditation. This technique is best described as letting go and generally termed *detachment*. While in the technique of the mental focus the meditator "attaches" himself to one thing in order both to focus awareness and to reduce the thought process, the technique of detachment allows the thought process to flow freely, without interruption or blocking. An attitude of indifference, or detached observation, is taken up. A thought arises. The meditator simply notes that fact and lets the thought disappear of its own accord, without thinking about the thought or following it. Whether a thought is pleasurable or painful, the meditator just lets it be, become, and die away.

Usually, detachment and the mental focus technique are combined. While the meditator lightly and repeatedly focuses on, say, counting to ten, thoughts will still sneak into awareness. Rather than tense up to block them by forcing attention back on counting, the meditator simply says, "A thought arises," to herself and returns to counting, as if the arising of a thought is quite natural and necessary but not serious enough to distract attention from the task at hand. She then returns to counting again. The perfection of the detachment technique lies in giving up counting and just sitting in awareness or doing nothing. Now awareness is free and independent, no longer relying on the crutch of counting or chanting. When this awareness is free even from the idea of meditation, the meditator has arrived.

The advantages of the technique of detachment—that it eliminates the tendency to become habituated to counting or to a mantra; reduces the tendency to block and deny our thoughts, feelings, and impulses; and tends to relax us more—have led some teachers to prefer it to the mental focus technique. Nevertheless, there is a danger in detachment. Directed toward habitual thoughts and responses, the attitude of detachment can sometimes become an attitude of indifference to the external world and other living beings. This is a mistake, may lead to apathy, and yields no good for ourselves or others. The essence of detachment is to become free of habits in order to become more aware. Becoming more aware, we become, not indifferent, but keenly sensitive to what is going on—in our heads as feelings and thoughts, and in the world as people and events whirl in joy, suffering, love, and ignorance.

The advantages of the mental focus technique lie in the fact that, by focusing on one thing, repeating and returning to it, the mind gains both intensity and relaxation of its general awareness, gradually eliminates or reduces the natural tendency to busy-ness and distraction, and increases its power to counteract old, destructive habits of living. In sum, the meditator is able to master his mind, to turn it to creative, rational, and moral commitments more frequently and steadily than before. Yet there is a genuine and often-seen danger in this technique, the tendency to become attached to or habituated to the use of one exclusive mental focus. When this occurs, the meditator has lost the psychological key to meditation—constantly freeing oneself from habits and unconsciously ingrained responses. The result is a kind of meditation fixation on the favorite mental focus and an inability to flexibly develop and apply the meditation attitude in and to various situations. The meditator who chants a mantra in every situation is an insecure and inflexible meditator, calming and reassuring himself by this habit rather than stabilizing and opening awareness to the need of the situation. The result, too often, is automatic or "technical" meditation, displaying a rigid, static quality. Meditation is a growth process, involving experimentation and stages of development in awareness. One mantra, or one mental focus, is not sufficient for maturation of the total self and in fact retards growth if it is the single and exclusive focus of attention. A maturing meditator, opening more and more to self-awareness and to world-awareness, will focus on several mantra or word-formulas that open up awareness, challenge the personality, and lead to action. Mantras abound in our lives: they are found in our deepest consciousness in words like *God, I, pain,* and *joy;* they are also found in the world in words like *help me, I love you,* and *save us all.* The meditator who meditates on these "words" of life will grow and help the world.

Meditation Practice in Everyday Life

Beginning meditators, in order to get the hang of it, usually must start out their practice by reserving two twenty-minute periods a day in which to meditate. For most people, meditation before breakfast, before supper, or about ninety-minutes before bedtime is easiest to manage in the daily schedule. Retiring to a quiet place in the house, the beginning meditator practices with the three B's, working the body into suitable postures, regulating and relaxing the breathing, and altering brain activity through concentration on a mental focus or the detachment of letting go and sitting in relaxed awareness.

It is by no means easy to make the time or create the place for meditation, since our days are usually structured by our own habits, by the habitual demands of others upon us in the house, and by the American notion that we must keep busy and avoid the feeling that we are doing nothing. At first, meditation looks and feels a lot like doing nothing. The rewards to the meditator quickly overcome any shyness or guilt about doing nothing, but his friends and family, wondering from outside the experience, may cause problems. The meditator must decide whether he has the right to briefly withdraw from involvement in order to practice meditation. It would be cruel to deny this right to another or to oneself. However, sometimes before sitting down to meditation, you have to put your foot down.

After two or three days of meditation, during which you work out the kinks in your situation, in your back, in your breathing, and in your brain, you will find it easy to identify the totally relaxed position and attitude of meditation and to reenter it after a few minutes of sitting. The mental experience will vary from time to time. Occasionally, you will hit the "groove" of relaxed awareness easily, like slowly diving into and floating in a pool of warm water, living and breathing quietly in the present moment. Sometimes, too, there will be difficulty, a sense of strain, of forcing yourself to go through the motions. Both experiences are equally valuable. The easy and pleasant meditation is its own reward and motivates us to try again to taste the pleasure and relaxation of meditation. The difficult times are valuable in that to continue to meditate when we do not feel like it strengthens the will. Such times are useful, also, in that we can see clearly what obstacles, usually of habit, are getting in our way. If we meditate even while feeling that we don't have the time, we may reconsider what we have done with our time or what other people are doing with "our time." Or we may be sitting and breathing quietly while our minds are racing around the day's business, unable or unwilling to focus on counting our breaths. Quiet breathing, well-centered in the stomach area of a relaxed body position, is two-thirds of meditation, regardless of the monkey-mind's control of our thoughts. After both easy and difficult beginning meditation periods, the meditator will almost always be more calm, more in control, more alert, and more energetic, for periods lasting from ten minutes to half a day.

If continued for weeks, twice-a-day meditation periods of perhaps twenty minutes each will produce results that are amazing and delightful for some, and interesting but mixed for others. Eventually, almost everyone slacks off, because this form of meditation becomes mechanical, habitual, and boring. That is, it ceases to be meditation, which is the breaking of habits by dwelling in a freeing, open, flexible, and relaxed awareness. We can see this backsliding often in people who practice Transcendental Meditation. The fault, in part, is in the TM method.

Twice-a-day meditation is most useful for beginners. It quickly provides a rewarding experience and produces confidence in the method and in oneself as a meditator. But it only places one on the first step of meditation. Having reached that plateau, the meditator must go to the next step if meditation is going to be real and effective in one's life.

The next plateau in meditation is to learn to meditate at will in more and more settings, under a variety of conditions, with mixed results in hour-by-hour everyday life. There are few daily tasks that cannot be approached with a meditation attitude, few activities in which it is impossible to apply body awareness, breathing skill, and mental techniques learned while doing sitting meditation in a controlled environment. Most of our daily environments are uncontrolled or uncontrollable in terms of the ideally effective and artificial environment we set up for sitting meditation. So we must learn to become aware of our bodies, breathing, and brains while walking and weeding, while talking and TV watching, while pinning diapers and pining for peace. We are living our lives in such moments; we can live more deeply, more efficiently, more fully if we bring to such moments the skills, insights, and balanced awareness of our meditation. Meditation is, at its best and most mature levels, not a matter of cloisters and closets, but a matter of life in the world. Meditation finally maintains itself and assists the world by becoming involved directly with pots and pans, people and purposes. Or, as one meditator put it centuries ago, "How marvelous this is! I carry water from the well. What a miracle! I chop wood for my fuel!"

CHAPTER 3

The Environment

Americans are highly skilled in
and fascinated by what might be called the technical approach
to life. Historically, we have been a pragmatic, technologically
innovative people, preoccupied with solving immediate problems by applying a technological solution. We take pride in and
reward the person who can "fix it," who knows how to do
something specific and practical. But we are not, at the same
time, a philosophical people, who would ask why this or that

should or should not be done. We also tend to be blissfully ignorant of the unintended consequences of our vast and remarkable abilities to do limited, specific things. It runs against our grain to pause before solving a problem in order to ask, "What effects will this solution, this technique, have on other problems, people, and the environmental network which contains the problem?" Trying to solve one problem alone and trying to apply a techniqe as if they existed in isolation from what surrounds and interacts with them, we get in over our heads, disrupting natural and human patterns and environments, which we then try to restore with still another "technological fix-it" response.

It is no surprise, therefore, that, in mocking defiance of our technological and educational superiority, we are faced with confusion and helplessness in "solving" pollution problems, in improving the physical and mental health of Americans, and in restoring order and balance to our social environment. It is also no surprise that meditation is beginning to appear more and more as another isolated technique, a set of fix-it steps to repair or polish the lives of Americans, just as we might take up tennis, pills, therapy, motorcycles, or jogging as a daily pick-me-up to lubricate the gears of body, emotion, and mind. But if meditation is absorbed into the American scene as another technique, for use by individuals in isolation from their own lives and from the American environment of needs and values, meditation will become, at best, a hobby of minor and tentative consequence. Reducing meditation to this status betrays its promise, falsifies its nature, and distorts its purpose.

The purpose of meditation is to open, to order, and to free human awareness so that people might live more abundantly with themselves, with others, and with the world. Its essential feature is a comprehensive process of unlearning mechanical or habitual responses and learning a new awareness in which we dwell fully and harmoniously on the earth. Its promise, in America, is to teach and show us that we are more than a herd of technically proficient people, frantically pursuing a kind of lonely and isolated happiness, whose lives and achievements are off-balance, incomplete, obscure, and self-consuming. A mature American meditation must go beyond technique and discover purpose and commitment; it must do this by going beyond a focus on individual-centered meditation into a sensitivity to and shaping of the community and environment in which the meditator lives, to which he responds, from which she draws her life energy, and to which we owe a great debt.

Meditation as Environmental Sensitivity: Awareness in a Coffee Cup

If we glance at the traditional image of the religious meditator as seen in a statue of the Buddha or a photograph of a Trappist monk, we see what appears to be the epitome of environmental and social isolation and insensitivity. The Buddha sits, eyes closed or almost closed, smiling peacefully, tuned to a transcendental theme or contemplating cosmic mystery, and detached from the world of humans and nature. The Christian monks have flocked to Egyptian deserts, Russian forests, or mountain eyries to pursue the highest goals they can imagine. The Hindu yogi retreats to a cave in the Himalayas, there to begin his meditation each day by mentally closing the gates of the senses so that no sight, sound, smell, or taste can play upon an awareness drawn inward. Jesus ventures into the wilderness for forty days to pray.

Such images of meditation do not, however, picture for us the full meaning and setting of meditation. The detachment achieved by these classical retreats is necessary, to some degree, for every meditator, in order to break away from interference or interruption and, more importantly, to temporarily separate the meditator from the community and environment in which habits have formed and been reinforced. Moving to a quiet place and time, the meditator achieves not an escape from the habitual world (that is only the means), but a confrontation with the naked self wherein meditation may do its work. In the quiet of meditation the sounds of the self may be heard, a listening that is aided considerably if the place of meditation is also quiet by being free of the noise of pots and pans, telephones, and other people. It is also in such settings that the "still, small voice" of the divine can be heard. Indeed, in the isolation and quiet of meditation, all sounds can be heard more clearly once the crusts of habit in perception, thought, and action have fallen away. Paradoxically, the quiet of meditation, in the traditional meditation environment, leads to perceptual and mental sensitivity. Having learned to hear and listen again, the meditator sometimes becomes acutely responsive to environmental stimuli.

If a meditator clings to solitude and quiet, the danger of quietism appears. To believe or act as if a quiet environment, which is usually an environment severely restricted in human interaction, is the best or necessary environment for meditation is to reach a meditative and moral dead end. While training in meditation requires some quiet time and place, meditation awareness is not such a delicate state that it can be only known and expressed in highly controlled and protected situations. Morally speaking, if meditation were such a delicate flower, it would be at best an art, but certainly not the moral and spiritual force and method it has shown itself to be in history. The highest moral traditions of East and West clearly suggest or assert that while we are becoming still and knowing God, we must also not be so far away or closed off that we cannot hear our neighbor's cry for joy or appeal for help. At its best, meditation will resensitize us to those human and other voices we have learned to hear not at all. Once we hear the sounds and voices again, and see with new eyes prepared in the quiet of meditation, we must go to work.

There is, then, a proper role to be played by closed-eye or "turtle" meditation, those exercises and times and places in which we withdraw temporarily into meditation with the goals of confronting and loosening our habitual selves and of learning to respond freely and harmoniously in awareness. Closed-eye meditation is a preparation for open-eye meditation, meditation in which we connect the awareness discovered in closed-eye meditation with the confusing, desperately real sights of the everyday world. We cannot cross Main Street, much less help our neighbor, unless our eyes are opened, responding free of habit and of self-absorption to the images of suffering, sickness, and sin. We *do* need the image and experience of the tranquil Buddha, but let us not close our eyes so often that we forget to behold the crucified body of Christ, in image and in experience.

Learning open-eye meditation means to literally open our eyes while meditating. After we are familiar with the "feel" of the relaxed state of alertness, it is important to open our eyes lightly and naturally, in order to avoid sleep or sluggishness and to restore connection with the immediate perceptual environment. We meditate in an environment which we cannot and should not ignore. Light, sound, temperature and humidity, living movements, and other factors are influencing the quality and success of the inner struggle and flow of meditation. Opening our eyes, ears, noses, and pores as well as our minds, we overcome the false view that meditation is a private, inner practice away from the world and prepare ourselves for the days in which we will meditate in the larger environment of people and everyday life. One of the Hindu scriptures decreed death as the penalty for anyone who even accidentally disturbed a yogi in his inner trance of meditation. One reason for this severity lies in the nature of profound closed-eye meditation: A sudden noise or disturbance can cause too rapid a return to ordinary consciousness and leave the yogi disoriented at best, psychotic at worst. American meditation, having little to do with the intense God-consciousness seen in Hinduism, must be an open-eye meditation, always in touch with the

immediate environment, not surprised or shocked by the in-
trusion of others, and ready to leap up alertly when action is
needed.

Open-eye meditation means more than just sitting with
eyes open in meditation. It points the way to living with eyes
open in all situations. Take the American custom, habit, and
ritual of starting a day with a cup of coffee and view the matter
with meditation-trained eyes. Because coffee contains stimu-
lants, such as caffeine, we can apply it to ourselves as a daily
(sometimes hourly!) technique for getting ourselves started,
overcoming the drowsiness of sleep, fatigue, or illness by inserting a bit of *stress* into the physical environment within. At
the same time, we may be drinking the coffee with family or
friends. The little rituals of coffee making, coffee serving, and
coffee drinking are, ironically, ways of inserting *relaxation* into
the interpersonal environment. Coffee has become for Americans the center of a partially conscious technology for producing alert relaxation or relaxed alertness, a quasi-meditation
state, we might say. The fact that the coffee ritual seems not
to have contributed to the betterment of people or society
should warn us that relaxed alertness is not enough, whether
it flows from coffee or from meditation. As compared with the
Japanese tea ritual, which was the center of centuries of innovation in personal manners, clothing, art, and architecture,
and which was guided and inspired by meditation principles
and the moral outlook of Zen Buddhism, our coffee ritual
seems still-born or trivial. We should start over, perhaps, by
emptying our coffee cups and not filling them again until we
can achieve that awareness, flowing from meditation, in which
the details, rhythms, and mood of coffee drinking combine to
reveal a special depth and fullness of things and of humanity.

As, with "open eyes," we drink coffee with our friends, the
coffee becomes, not a stimulant in a mechanical technology,
but the emblem of friendship and the gift of nature. Sensitized
in meditation, we may come to savor and respect the click of

cups, the aroma of the brew, the colors dancing about, the silences of people, and the fullness of time. If our kidneys hold out long enough, we might learn to love, accept, and respect each other and the planet—by drinking coffee together!

Open-eye meditation is meditation that recognizes that as individuals we are never separate from the environment in which we meditate. Constant interaction on many levels between ourselves and our world cannot be ignored if meditation is to be accomplished and flow into the world. Foolish and self-deceiving are the meditators who neglect to note the influences and pressures of their immediate perceptual environment on the possiblity and quality of their meditation practice. Normally ignored features of the spaces in which we live, such as lighting and shadows, the rumble of traffic on the streets, body odors, the flow of air in a room, or the tightness of clothes on the skin, steadily become more noticed, more *present* to us in meditation awareness.

Probably the keenest difference between ordinary awareness and meditation awareness, as responses to the immediate, perceived environment, appears when a meditator, in meditation, hears another human voice. Ordinarily, we screen out the tension often underlying the words uttered by others, but in meditation awareness this tension becomes very clear, and it sounds almost like wordless screaming. The fact that meditation produces such extreme sensitivity in part accounts for the traditional meditators' flight to desert silences. But it is also necessary that American meditators in these days face this fact of their environment (for few of us can "go to the desert") and do two things. First, they must learn to persist in meditation awareness even when it reveals painful and deeply disturbing "vibrations" in the immediate environment. They must remain steady, calm, and alert, absorbing and letting go these signals from an outside world which is also inside. They must not, to escape painful stimuli, block them out, but reinforce the will to remain steady and aware. They must not turn from the sound or sight, revealed in meditation, of the subtle agony of others. To turn away is to protect our own awareness by screening out reality in the belief that we cannot "take it." To turn away is also to abandon the world and other people, and to refuse our obligation to help others.

Meditation reveals, both painfully and pleasantly, previously concealed or habitually ignored features of the world in which we live. We can see both sunsets and suffering more acutely than before. We should not turn from either, nor sit passively in quietism as we see. In open-eyed meditation awareness, a time for action will emerge in its fullness as the need and opportunity in and of the environment appear to the aware and ready meditator. Sensitive to the environment as a place of need and as a field of opportunity, the maturing meditator perceives different or creative ways for changing the environment or some feature of it and possesses a power and perspective for making change. No doubt, some changes will emerge first within the environment that the meditator has direct control over, such as her meditation room or the meditation "space" she carries with her and recreates each time she moves into meditation. If she takes an ordinary daily activity, such as drinking coffee, and approaches it each time with meditative, open-eyed, and active sensitivity, she can transform it into a ritual that supports calm awareness for herself and for others. More extensive alterations in the environment may deepen the meditator's own ability to meditate as well as subtly influence others. American homes, for example, are commonly noisy. She can quiet hers down, by seeing into the habits producing noise and modifying them. One "noise" in the home results from the habit of covering the walls with paintings and objects. Quickly, they are no longer seen by members of the family because they cancel each other out by their numbers and conflict. It is better for meditation, more economical, and more satisfying to have only a few objects and paintings displayed at one time and place. Store the excess away, rotate the stock season by season, and the objects will come alive again, as will the now-dynamic or changing environment.

The effects of environmental sensitivity and alertness can quickly be seen by comparing a Christian or Buddhist monastery, with its simplicity of decoration approaching austerity, with an American home, cluttered with forgotten objects, stuffed with masses of furniture, and sprouting gadgets everywhere. Yet these same houses are barren of rhythms and change in color, sound, aroma, and taste. They tend to dull the senses, cramp the bodies, and bore the minds of their occupants, who turn on the television, fall asleep, go to a movie, or take a trip in their cars to revive themselves. Our houses are the easiest environments to shape for human purposes and the most influential, yet they become prisons, filled with mindless routine, dulling overstimulation, hostile and unknown objects, and a gnawing yearning for something better—a new painting, a new house, a new life? Masters and conquerors of the American wilderness, we cannot shape 1500 square feet to support, express, teach, and satisfy our fullest and deepest humanity. Open-eyed meditators, as they steadily mature, will change their immediate environments, however; with that change, they change themselves and others.

The Meditation Community: Alternatives to the Monastery

At first glance, contemporary Americans who follow the paths of meditation must do so alone, as isolated individuals, under poor conditions, since we lack both the supportive society and the ideal environmental conditions of the monastery or meditation center. Those of us who have been fortunate enough to meditate in a Christian monastery, a Buddhist *zendo*, or a Hindu *ashram*, abroad or one of the few available in America, are keenly aware of the advantages of monastery environments and society in helping the meditation process and in focusing on the change in the self that accompanies it. Hopefully, more such places will be available for short-term training and practice in the future. Better yet would be meditation centers and houses adapted to the needs and limitations of the American way of life.

Monasteries at their best are places of training, practice, and service, centered around a spiritual or meditation discipline or way of life, guided by high goals and teachers who know the path, and committed to educational interaction with the world. In the Christian West, monasteries were the forerunners of universities, places of scholarship, technological innovation, cultural preservation, and social criticism. In some parts of Asia today, particularly in Buddhist Southeast Asia, the monastery or temple continues to serve similar social purposes, not yet supplanted by secularized universities controlled by and geared to the values of the modern economy and the nationalist state. The trend of modernization, however, seems to run against monasteries as institutions so long as the larger society remains secular and can avoid major continuing instability, breakdowns, or chaos.

From the point of view of meditation practice in America, monasteries or their more informal and smaller alternatives, meditations centers or houses, would provide a protected place and, more importantly, a gathering of people in community for the practice and exploration of meditation itself. While meditation is primarily a matter of the individual working in and upon himself, others are needed to guide, support, and share meditation practice. Sitting down to meditation is easier, less troubled, and more successful when done with others, be they two or two hundred. The presence of like-minded others seems to strengthen the will to meditate. The experience of others, when shared freely and kindly, encourages the meditator, reveals new angles and dead ends, provides models, and helps us avoid getting "puffed up" with pride as we progress. The awareness and strength of friends is ours also in the inevi-

table times when we run into very specific difficulties in meditation: when meditation becomes dry, "spacy," disorienting,
ecstatic, or psychologically and morally disruptive, as it does
when we advance into deeper confrontation with the self and
uncover more and more layers of habit, ignorance, insensitivity, and fear in our consciousness.

The monastic pattern of life, furthermore, enhances the
prospects for tension reduction and concentration on the work
of meditation. The key principles of the monastic life are simplicity and order. The basic human necessities of food, shelter,
and clothing are provided only to the extent necessary to support the limited, intense lives of monks and nuns. There is
little ornamentation, individuality, expressiveness, or luxury in
the monastic meditators' life necessities compared to those of
the outside world. While this simplicity has a moral dimension
in the monastery's refusal to exploit the outside world by gathering and hoarding wealth, its functional purpose is psychological—to clarify and simplify life equally for all in the
monastery so that they may focus on their personal depth
without undue distraction by the surface refinements and com-
parisons of individual and social existence.

The traditional vows of monks—poverty, chastity, and
obedience—similarly are commitments to simplify life from
distracting complications. In the vows we tend to see only a
denial of human desires to possess things, to seek pleasure
and possess others, and to maintain independent control over
our lives. The monk sees the forsaking of these desires of the
self as a way to free the self from complications and entangle-
ments that obscure his work upon himself. In order to gain
mastery of his habitual self, body, emotion, and mind, he must
set these "natural" desires aside, at least temporarily, but perhaps for a lifetime.

The monastic pattern also tends to be a highly ordered one,
with a more or less fixed annual and daily schedule of limited
activities. There is little improvisation or idiosyncrasy in

monastic life, for at least three reasons. First, idiosyncratic behavior is usually a matter of an individual acting out of desire or impulse. Since the aim of every monk is to bring the fickle habitual self under control, such deviations from a norm of dress, work, or schedule must be controlled for the sake of the monk himself. Second, improvisation by one or a few monks disturbs the concentration of others, who may or must deal with the difference as an interruption. Third, the predictability and regularity of the monastic pattern of time, ritual, clothing, social greetings, and so on provide a larger framework of mutual, shared control of the meditation environment to enhance the prospect that each monk or meditator will feel secure in his daily life. Of course, the order of the monastic pattern can become or be seen as monotony in a bad sense, or can result in an oppressive and impotent system, unless the community constantly reaffirms and experiences the ordering of life as the prerequisite for freedom, trust, and mutual support.

A casual visitor to a monastery or controlled meditation center may, understandably, wonder how the quiet, unhurried, similarly dressed occupants can find any meaning in a life empty of diversion, excitement, high jinks, and individualism. Conversely, the monk too long in the simple order of the monastery may wonder how the frantic, interrupted, "pillar-to-post" lives of outsiders can provide meaning or peace or focus. The monk and the visitor are habituated to their own worlds of environmental stimuli, social interaction, and values, of course. If they both were free of this habituation or prejudice, they could more readily pass between the two worlds, bringing the goods of each to bear upon the other. From the larger perspective of human nature and destiny, the two worlds are one and should remain in dialogue, just as closed-eye and open-eye meditation must interact. We must observe, however, that in contemporary America it is more often the monk than the outsider who is willing to walk in two worlds.

For the American meditator, the monastery environment is rarely accessible or is not a genuine option. But while we cannot take ourselves to a nunnery or monastery, or even a less formal meditation center, we *can* learn lessons from the monastic pattern of life and society and experimentally test the lessons in our own patterns of life and in our interactions with other people.

We do not need to live in a monastery in order to regulate our involvement with other people in ways to enhance their and our own better self. It is imperative that meditators in the world choose their associations mindfully. Too often the virtue of American friendliness and openness, our readiness to be available to and influenced by others, results in mere politeness as a facade over the tension that certain people produce in us almost by osmosis. There are times when the meditator (even a monk) must avoid or leave the presence of people with "bad vibes," destructive people, hate-filled people. It does no good, for ourselves or for others, if we appear to condone evil, foolish, or delusioned acts, thoughts, or emotions in others or in ourselves. We must seek, rather, the good and the wise, when and wherever we find them. On entering a town, a factory, a school, a church, or a meeting, we should ask, "Who is the wisest, freest, most peaceful person here?" The question, if asked aloud, will startle everyone. The answer will more likely come from our own sensitive observations, and when it does, we can test it out by associating with and learning from these people, who probably are looking for us, too. Last, these people who benefit others because of who they are probably are not conscious meditators, rarely occupy positions of power and title, almost always are children or oldsters, wear simple clothes, and claim no merits for themselves.

As good people are found, the meditator should practice open-eye meditation in their presence. We should practice the three B's in relaxed awareness as we interact, whether sitting, walking, talking, or listening. Establishing ourselves in meditation under these favorable conditions of personal encounter, we will learn from the good and prepare for committing ourselves to be with the not-so-good, the fearful, the distressed, the hate-filled, and the unlovable in order to help *them* by being who we are. Just as we can draw upon the strength of the good, our secret friends, so can we be drawn upon as the strength for the not-so-good, our needy neighbors, even our open enemies. Monks can do no more, and often do less because of their isolation.

The essential secret of the monastic community is that each member is allowed, encouraged, and expected to be fully and deeply human, and an end in himself. The monastery pattern of life, by stripping people and the environment down to the essentials, enhances the prospect that no one will be viewed or acted upon as an instrument of another human will or desire, as a functionary, as a thing. This refusal to treat people as things is the achievement of the monastery, the human core of the great religions, the first principle of ethics, the criterion of friendship. In being with others, the meditator at large in American society can reach for this attitude by applying meditation to situations where the temptation arises to "use" others for the sake of our own interests or the interests of others. It requires a certain tension in the body, a feeling of closing down part of our self, when we are about to use another. The meditator, more sensitive to these alternations in body and mind, can interrupt the posture of exploitation, and take on another posture and attitude.

Allowing others to be themselves does not mean that the meditator in the world is permissive, anarchical, and of the view that we should follow or be allowed to follow our impulses or do our own thing. Well-acquainted with the impulses and habits of his ordinary self, a meditator can recognize the inauthentic masquerades of others who try to assert or create their personality as a substitute for discovering their true humanity. Meditators, like monks, must allow, expect, and help others to become more deeply human, more free, courageous, honest, trusting, and loving. This often means that meditators are impatient, impolite, or even crude when dealing with some manifestations of false or shallow or abusive humanity. It is true, however, that more often their response is indirect and gentle, giving rise to the notion that meditators are soft on or tolerant of human failing in others, but harsh on themselves and their friends.

Finally, Americans who are meditators at large should not be overly concerned with the absence of a classic, protected community of meditators within easy reach for themselves. While it is true that such communities provide the optimum setting for meditation training and for a few people who will choose seclusion and a focused community as a lifestyle, it is also true that most of us are "worldlings," who, if we persevere in meditation in spite of the obstacles of our society and environments, will gain a depth, strength, flexibility, and expression of meditation that cannot be matched by the monk, whose new self has ripened in the carefully controlled setting of the monastery. The worldling who has won the struggle for humanity in the tumult of life is worth more to the world, it must be said, than those who have had all the advantages of monastic life.

The Meditation Teacher: Growing without a Guru

Traditional meditation schools stress the importance, and sometimes the necessity, of a spiritual director (as in Christianity), a *guru* (as in Hinduism), or a *roshi* (as in Eastern Buddhism) in the guidance and protection of the meditation process. These advanced souls, from whom the meditator receives instruction, correction, and confirmation as he moves through the psychological, moral, and religious struggles and stages of meditation, are also the models of the quality of life to which the meditator aspires. The director's words and thoughts, the guru's extra-normal powers, the roshi's silences and physical movements—all reveal a total state of being, of full humanity, of perfection, to the struggling meditator. Having traveled the path, ascended the heights, and seen the vision, the teacher is seen by disciples and students as hero, physician, sage, and parent. Especially in the Asian traditions of Hinduism and Buddhism, we can see the immense authority and prestige of the meditation teacher, whose disciples became his "children," whose feet were called blessed, and whose presence radiated peace, bliss, and rays of truth.

The perfected meditation master was not a mere teacher of technique or the possessor of special understandings. He was the perfect model and expression of a total way of being and relating, teaching as much by his silences as by his words, as much by the way he related to children, pain, and eating as by his discourses before the learned assembly of his students. He was meditation itself, the perfect expression of relaxed awareness, of peaceful and penetrating consciousness. His eyes bore into the souls of his students, his hands healed their brokenness, and his voice was like subtle nectar. Such is the testimony of the students and of others, too, who came into the "presence" to see "this teacher who everybody talks about" and went away soothed, disturbed, or amazed. Interestingly, when Asian meditation students first read about Jesus, their first response is often to liken him to a meditation master, since he seems to have had a similar effect upon his disciples and audiences.

We in America today seldom, if ever, will encounter a meditation master, much less have the chance to study with and, more important, live with one. They are an endangered species. There are plenty of people about the land who seem happy to let us believe they are gurus or masters, but the best meditation teachers in America will be the first to defuse our will to believe that they are perfect. Meditators should be on guard against their own desire to know and experience a meditation master, for the desire can give birth to its object. We can easily deceive ourselves by creating our own masters and gurus out of yearning, perhaps by the same route that we create stars in sports, entertainment, politics, and other areas. At the same time, we should guard against false masters and teachers. We can recognize them by their self-advertisement, wealth, and pride. A self-styled meditation teacher or master with enormous ego, with a kind of tension-filled dynamism and appeal, is at best immature and at worst self-deceiving and dangerous. These characters are not numerous, but the few that are around do seem to get around quite well.

The traditional criteria for judging a perfect master still hold true. Ideally, only another master could recognize a master. This led to the system of lineage, where a master would certify which of his students would continue as his spiritual sons and heirs. We must ask, then, of a possible master, "Who was his teacher?" But this criterion of lineage is not enough (for sons can turn "bad" and lose the way), so it is necessary to inquire into and observe the master's moral conduct and character ("by their fruits you shall know them") and his students' conduct and character. Further, even if we find an authentic master, he may not fit our need or personality. If we do not "resonate," we must search elsewhere.

Whether we are searching for a guru in sixth-century India or twentieth-century America, however, finally the teacher of meditation is our own best and deepest self. Hinduism recognized this in its concept of the supreme teacher within, who awakens us to the need for meditation in the first place and who, when uncovered at last, confirms the achievement. The concept of the Kingdom of God being within us may mean much the same. Christ may not come into our hearts, but *be there* all the time, waiting for us, stirring our hearts into the awareness and actions wherein he can be seen at last. With less presumption, we can at least know that the urge to take up meditation rises from within us, that there is something about meditation or meditators that draws us to it or them, and there is something about ourselves that responds or grows in the context of meditation. Sometimes, it is our ego that grows ("I had a very successful meditation today"; "I am more relaxed and aware than Jack or Mary"; "If I keep this up, I could be a master, Buddha, or saint someday"). But often a clear and unmistakable feeling or thrill comes over the meditator, indicating progress and leaps in growth and depth. These are signs from the teacher within and can be trusted. But we should not think or talk about them if to do so makes us proud. Easily, too easily, these signals are swept up into our habitual ways of looking at and owning our achievements, whereupon the signals become toys of the monkey-mind or trophies of our self-regard. Since there will be times when the thrill does not come, after months of meditation, it is best not to look for them or hold on to them. We should just smile at them and return to meditation.

Learning meditation without a master is difficult, but possible. Learning meditation without instruction is virtually impossible. If there are no teachers around who can provide basic instruction and answer questions satisfactorily, read the many books available. Do not rely on just one teacher or just one book; encounter and test as many as you can. The problem with books and teachers as instructional sources is that only one is too narrow, too many are confusing, and they all fill your head (and your meditation!) with great expectations. Keep cool, keep your head, while you are practicing and experimenting with meditation.

The American who meditates long enough or the few who are "natural meditators" will eventually reach a crossroads. The signposts are the desire to sit for long periods of time in quiet meditation, irritation with your self or the environment, a feeling that you must make a critical decision about radically changing your lifestyle, or even a hankering after the "true" life in a monastery in India or in San Francisco. These signs may also appear in painful or deeply disturbing ways, as the conflict between your old, habitual self and your emerging meditation self takes on the appearance of a battle, disturbs your sleep, and confuses your days. Unless you are "destined" for the monastery, called into that form of life by the feeling that, without going, you will be less than what you are, you should remain and make everyday life your field of practice. Throwing yourself into the world, turning from a private, inner practice toward a practice in which you tranform your life in the events and routines of going about your business, living more and more each day in mindfulness and centering, you will grow strong and achieve satisfaction. For most of us, it is probably the case that, if we are mature meditators, the world before our eyes needs us more than we need the monastery.

Gradually, having transformed meditation into a practice of everyday life, we will discover that there is an abundance of friends of peace around us, splendid moments and places for meditation, and teachers aplenty. If we get lost or dry in our practice, we should relax and let a child, a cat, a tree, or a dandelion pushing through the pavement to reach the sun be our teacher, model, and deepest protector.

CHAPTER 4

The Moral Dimensions

Meditation in the contemporary American scene presents itself as a technique for, of, and by individuals. The focus on technique is congenial to our how-to-do-it, practical orientation, but neglects the questions of value and purpose that must be asked about any technique. Furthermore, focus on the individual can neglect the interpersonal and relational dimensions of meditation practice. While meditation appears to be a lonely endeavor of the isolated individual in privacy, aiming to achieve an inner or self-oriented state or goal, it is also true that meditation occurs in a context or environment of human needs and values and that meditation results in practices and powers of no little significance for others and for America.

Meditators are members of a community to which they are related in moral awareness and reciprocal obligation. Just as the communities of others in the family, institution, or country are obliged to allow or tolerate the individual pursuits of meditators, so, too, meditators are obliged to assess their impact on others and to seek the good and health of the community through positive acts. Too often the individualistic foci of meditation and of American life combine to conceal or obscure the moral dimensions of the life assisted by or centered in meditation. If meditation is to be of significance in America and to reach maturity in the meditator, however, its moral dimensions must be outlined and fully understood. Only then can the promise, value, and limits of meditation practice become clear.

The Place of Morality in Traditional Meditation

Much in contrast with the picture of meditation as a technique available to anyone for private use is the traditional view of meditation evidenced in Western and Eastern religious communities. Traditionally, meditation training was available only after a preliminary period of moral training, during which the meditation instructors would assess the novices' moral stature and prescribe a program of moral behavior and development. Only after moral education and mastery was the novice initiated into the method of inner education and self-mastery called meditation.

Although there existed variations from community to community and from teacher to teacher, generally the moral rule or discipline consisted of vows and practices of poverty, chastity, obedience to and faith in the teacher, and regulations for communal life. While these moral standards and practices had a practical dimension in that they served to simplify the individual's and the community's life to the degree necessary for concentration on meditation and spiritual work, they were also an arena of testing oneself and others in the art of self-mastery. Unless the outer, more easily observed behavior and impulses of the meditator could be mastered, it was unlikely that the inner contest could succeed and true mastery over emotional and mental habits be achieved.

Needless to say, some meditators and monks would achieve control only over outer acts and behavior. Because they were lazy or their teacher was lazy, they might not proceed to the inner work of meditation, breaking the bodily, emotional, and mental habits of the old self and achieving an inner freedom that would issue forth into enlightened and compassionate acts. Others might fail to move inward because of false pride in their ability to control their behavior and to appear as one of the truly righteous, meticulous in the details of their actions and composure but ignorant of the perversions of spiritual pride and "one-upmanship."

The primary reason for a probationary period, in which the moral capacity of the novice was both assessed and shaped, lay in the traditional view that meditation was not merely a neutral technique, but a means to power. If the force of a well-trained will were applied only to the meditator, there would be less reason to take the precautions of probation. But, in the traditional view, the process of meditation led to specific powers to help or harm others, and thus meditation was necessarily a moral matter. A meditator of skill, it was believed, could direct the power of a mastered mind to healing the minds and bodies of others; conversely, the same power, in a skilled but immoral meditator, could be used for selfish, manipulative, or destructive ends. Thus the power gained through meditation was to be reserved for the few who could pass strict moral tests. The moral point of view was that the knowledge of human nature gained in meditation was a powerful knowledge, and such power should be given only to the morally strong and mature.

Meditation was not merely a path of the isolated soul in search of God and wholeness. It was a force in the world and could transform the relationships, including power relationships, between people. Moral inspection and training were absolutely essential if the transforming powers of meditation were to work for goodness, for the good of all rather than the good of the meditator. Indeed, the final test of the maturity and depth of a traditional meditator was, in all traditions East and West, the capacity to transcend self and go to work self-sacrificially for the benefit of others. The absence of selfishness, or humility, and the will to benefit others, or love, were the highest and final test of the Christian or Buddhist meditator. That not a few passed the test is evident in the lives and dedication to the world's needs of hundreds of men and women through the centuries, across the planet.

The absence of moral training and tests is one of the startling features of much contemporary American meditation. While the morally structured life of meditation can be observed in teachers and communities of meditation still close to their religious roots, more often than not meditation or quasi-meditation techniques are presented as self-help tools to be used for private and vague ends or for purposes of worldly success: better grades (rather than knowledge and learning), more efficient work (rather than more happy and whole workers), higher skill levels in sports (rather than more wholesome sports and players), or decreased dependency on drugs (rather than the creation of a healthy person). The more general and moral purposes remain parenthetical, a bit vague, or unsellable in a culture whose moral authorities and principles have lost their audiences, their clarity, and their clout. Meditation, the art and science of overcoming the structure of habits we call *ego* or *me*, is presented so as to appeal to the ego by promising greater energy and skill in fulfilling its goals ("Want to improve your tennis? Take up meditation!") Freed from the guidance, insight, and constraint of moral education, meditation becomes a technique serving confused and conflicting ends.

It is, perhaps, too much to hope that meditation will once again be married to inspiring and disciplined moral frameworks, ways of life, and communities, although such interactions are not totally absent and can be seen in the overtly religious communities in which meditation is practiced. Nevertheless, meditation can be taught and shaped in such a way as to minimize its perversion if meditation teachers become morally sensitive and alter their presentation of meditation in general and techniques in particular. Certain techniques and exercises that lead to beneficial effects should be stressed, while other techniques should be eliminated if they do not pass the test. The test is: Does this exercise lead *directly* to seeing, willing, and doing good for others?

Finally, each meditator should be obliged and should oblige herself to turn over the fruits of meditation, as soon as they appear in the meditation process, to others. To keep or use them for herself benefits no one, not even the meditator, who may be vain and alienated from others by her special powers. The meditator may be more energetic than others, for example; this energy should be given over to the proper use of others, unless the meditator needs it to support her basic life necessities. It becomes obvious, even with this simple example, that the meditator is faced with moral calculation and reasoning as she benefits from and seeks to benefit others as a result of meditation. She may gain more energy by meditation but allow that energy to be drawn upon by others who would apply it to doubtful or shameful purposes. If a meditator becomes a more effective worker through meditation's effects on his attention, energy, or health, he is not freed from responsibility for the work he is doing in terms of its effects on others. A soldier may become a more effective killer through meditation, but meditators should prefer to be soldiers of and for humanity.

Meditation as a Way to Moral Sensitivity

Although contemporary American meditators are seldom directed and shaped by explicit moral concerns and education, they are not immune to a significant moral process that unfolds in a regular practice of meditation. Just as meditation produces increased sensitivity to the environment, so does it generally result in increased moral sensitivity and increased capacity for moral action.

Meditation can be described as a dehabituation or deautomatization process, in that our regular, semi-conscious habits of body, emotion, and mind tend to become clearer, more conscious, and more available for change. Becoming aware of our habitual routines presupposes a dimension of ourselves that is aware of our habits and free from them to a useful degree. Meditation opens us to alternatives of body posture, emotion, and thinking patterns; frees us momentarily from the habit or habits that may be restricting our self-awareness or sensitivity to others; and provides the space in which to accept our faults and firm our wills to change.

Moral sensitivity is the awareness of alternatives of action and feeling. In the quiet, calm sitting of meditation we can see the possibility of a depth of satisfaction in contrast to our usually frantic, busy lives. In that quiet we can also question, intuitively, our ordinary lives and achieve the faith that matters can, or even should, be different. In a small way, we may become sensitive to a little habit that we overlook and begin to ask, calmly, why we do it. Continuing in the quiet of meditation, the meditator often finds the answer arising: "You do not have to do that." This is the beginning of a moral situation. We are faced with the choice of continuing or ceasing a habit, but facing the choice occurs in the self-controlled atmosphere of meditation, not in the rush of the day, when it can be easily put aside, or not in a meeting with a friend, whose advise we usually reject unless we are already inwardly prepared to follow it.

In meditators already engaged in assessing the moral commitments of their lives, who are seeking some vision and reality of the good life, the clarification of their habits may snowball into a choice, not to eliminate a bad habit or two, but to change the whole style, substance, and direction of their lives. This experience can be so deep that they feel born again. Unless this experience is worked out and practiced daily, however, it becomes only a memory. To change our life requires constant and forgiving vigilance toward the self. Meditation is a way to such vigilance, for in meditation we come closest to facing and being faced by ourselves, in our pettiness, our pride, and our promise.

Meditation not only leads to greater self-awareness, important as that is to moral sensitivity. Meditation, rightly viewed, leads to self-acceptance. The meditator who cannot overlook, or set aside, troubling aspects of herself while she is meditating cannot proceed in meditation, since she gets uptight or wrapped up too much in the details of herself. Often, after a meditation practice is well-established, the meditator will have sessions that are disturbing or painful confrontations with herself. She may get caught up in a train of thoughts leading to self-blaming or excessive self-criticism. When these arise, she must allow them to appear and not try to block their expression, but she should also not let them interrupt or break the calm flow of meditative thought. She must smile in self-acceptance as they appear and, inevitably, disappear. It is a matter of remaining relaxed and aware, and dwelling in the pure awareness, without focusing or getting caught up by what passes over the mirror of awareness.

Furthermore, meditation leads to receptivity—the ability to sense another person's posture, or primary response to ourself and a situation—and to sympathy—the ability to step into others' shoes, to see with their eyes. To become sensitive to the feelings and reactions of others, sometimes in spite of what they say, may be a distraction to our inward meditation. If someone is subtly crying for help or clarity, those cries can penetrate into meditation that is focused for the moment on ourself. Rather than run away to pursue our private meditation, we should at proper times direct awareness at those cries, determine their weight, and take action. Generally, if meditation is open-eyed, the meditator walks among others, antenna out, sensitive to what is going on beneath the habitual and concealing surface performances of social and interpersonal interaction.

An open-eyed meditation, tuned into the world and not closed off from it, evolves in abilities to sympathize, to identify with and know objects and people by grasping them from within. In meditation the habitual barriers we erect against objects and people are loosened, our senses and skin become transparent to external stimuli, and we lose the feeling of being separate from the environment and others. While the meditation increases our awareness of others, it also decreases the tensions we have with and about others. Being both more alert and more relaxed, the meditator can become more perceptive of good and bad, pleasant and unpleasant features of others, but more comfortable in their presence. This results in fewer harsh feelings and attitudes, along with less tendency to flee the presence of certain people who usually might be judged disreputable, offensive, or even evil. Rather than being harsh and judgmental with others, meditators are harsh, if at all, with themselves. This is the beginning of moral wisdom.

Last, there is sufficient evidence to believe that a maturing meditation practice results in strengthening the virtues necessary for moral action. The physical discipline of the meditator may subtly assist in the development of courage and endurance. The resolve to sustain meditation through periods of dryness and to persist in spite of inner and outer obstacles may lead to strengthened self-confidence and a healthy, will power. The inevitable shortcomings and failures during meditation and connected with it, combined with the larger, gentle awareness of meditation, will perhaps result in that rare moral virtue, a sense of humor, along with an appreciation for patience, since meditation, like moral commitment, is a prolonged, slowly unfolding process of growth that can rarely be hastened by the application of a quick-fix technique. In the long run of our individual moral careers and in the moral struggle of America, these are the virtues needed by all.

Morality as the Form and Face of Meditation

Accustomed as we are to viewing meditation as a technique, we often neglect to ask critically and carefully what the technique is for, what it should be applied to. Indeed, so fascinating are the details and experiences of practicing meditation that the meditator is even tempted to view the practice as an art, an intrinsically satisfying and challenging end in itself. Nevertheless, as meditation advances in the life process of an individual, questions arise as to the direction and purpose of meditation. Sometimes as meditation becomes tiresome, routine, or a burden, or as few benefits are received from the practice, the meditator is tempted to quit: "I don't seem to enjoy it anymore," or "It doesn't seem to work anymore." At other times the meditator loses a sense of meaning in the practice and is lured by curiosity or outside influence into taking up another hobby in the search for "Experience." Unless meditation practice is based in a repeated moral commitment to self and others, these periods of questioning, dryness, and boredom which always come into meditation will likely result in the breakaway of thousands of people who once did meditation enthusiastically but who now throw their energies in other directions.

When we work in meditation to make ourselves freer and more capable of sensitive relationships to our self, to the world, and to other people, we are also laying the groundwork for our moral being. When we act with moral sensitivity with and toward others, as well as with and toward ourselves, we are expanding meditation beyond a private technique or art, connecting ourselves to the world and community, and discovering meaning in meditation. The two—meditation and morality—go together as each reaches for its perfection. Meditation without morality, without connection to the world and other people, is empty, shrunken, or self-destructive. Morality without meditation, without calm self-mastery and self-awareness, is obedience to habit or authority, the cause of self-righteousness, a mockery of freedom, and a sign of moral immaturity.

Rather than view meditation as a technique in search of a morality, in which case any morality might do, we should view meditation as a way of relation, in which our educated awareness opens into freer, responsive, and bold relationship with ourselves, the world, and others. The higher moralities, based on wisdom and compassion, are maps of the terrain as it opens to view during meditation. Morality gives form and detail to the life made self-aware through meditation, so that meditation becomes more than a technique to improve a tennis game, a means to "recharge the psychic batteries" so we can "drive" harder in the world, or a tool for "making it" for "Number One." Meditation that is morally directed and motivated is a method for learning to be fully at home in relation with others, to fulfill our promise as persons in and for community, to love your neighbor as yourself. Meditation without a sense of relationship to others, without a moral insight and obligation, is a meditation difficult to sustain for ourselves, retarded in its potential, and a symptom of smallness of soul.

After the first few weeks of meditation practice, when the

first pleasant fruits of meditation have been tasted and consumed, beginners reach a plateau where meditation does not
result in increased energy, alertness, and tranquility. For those
who seek only these pleasant results in meditation, their practice tends to go downhill over the following months. Such
pleasure seekers will soon cease to be meditators. They have
reached the threshold of the second stage of meditation and
turned back. The second stage can be reached only by a moral
decision to commit oneself to the process of meditation because of what it promises in self-knowledge and in power to
help others. The meditator then continues meditation because
of this commitment alone, for it is certain that the self-knowledge gained will be bittersweet and that one's meager, medita-
tion-produced powers to help and fully be with others will be
sorely tested. A mechanical meditation will not sustain the
course of self-confrontation and helping others. Only a firm
and clear will to know oneself and to do the good will carry the
meditation on. The meditation will *then* support, strengthen,
and comfort the will power of the meditator.

It should be obvious that meditation is an effort and practice that draws forth and draws back upon our whole being. We
may enter the practice out of confused motives of curiosity, the
desire to relax, or the promise of assistance in some narrow
aspect of our lives. But after the initial period of learning
technique and receiving the benefits of increased ease and
alertness, we discover, through a sense of uneasiness or in a
flash, that meditation pushes us to change our lives. Revealing
our emotional storms, it raises the possibility of a balanced
emotional life. Restoring our energies, it poses the questions
of where, how, when, and why we can and should apply these
energies. In sum, meditation quickly presents us with a series
of choices and reveals to us our moral nature and freedom.
Meditation shows us its and our moral face. It is not a technique, comparable to other techniques, nor is it an art alone,
a therapy for adjusting to the world as it is or a simple path to

"natural" happiness. It is, rather, a method of seeking, knowing, and living the truth and the good, accompanied by risk, confusion, pain, and darkness, as are other ways to truth and goodness.

Meditation for Christians, Jews, and Other Friends of the Good

America is now the scene of a bewildering variety of meditation teachers, systems, techniques, and viewpoints. Yet meditation appears to be adrift. Now connected with a Hindu swami, next week isolated into a mental-health technique, here appearing as a tool of professional athletes to sharpen their combative edge, now visible as an experiment in the rehabilitation of drug abusers-meditation wanders, homeless, through the land.

Until meditation is taken into the lives of morally clear and committed Americans, those who share a common vision and experience of morality of the highest order, meditation will remain a resource for the few and a curiosity for the many. It is time, then, that seekers of the good, especially religious people living in America, should carefully consider the experimental possibility of practicing meditation and of deepening meditation through the moral commitment, clarity, and experience that is theirs.

Religious education in America, in spite of its self-criticized weaknesses and shortfalls, does provide the moral framework and training once provided, in varying degrees, by monks and masters. The American moral emphasis on the responsibility of adults for their own behavior and inner conscience, although it can lead to the excess of permissiveness and moral anarchy, does create many individuals who are as watchful over their own moral behavior, as scrupulous in mastering their desires, and as wise in moral reasoning, as any monk of ancient times. In America, without doubt and in spite of our worst self-images, there live and work a hopeful number of people who already have gained moral maturity, as evidenced in their self-sacrifice, concern for right and justice, and efforts to perfect themselves and help others. These are the people, above all others, for whom meditation is meant and through whom it can realize its potential as a way to self-knowledge and to the love which can make all things new and whole again.

There is no conflict between meditation and moralities which seek truth, preserve reason, and value freedom, justice, and love. Meditation is perfected in such moralities and, in turn, empowers and deepens them. As a discipline of the whole self—body, emotions, mind, and actions—meditation tends to work upon the whole person, allowing no habitual separation of ourselves or our morality into compartments. Our morality, and our personhood, must be whole and unified, involving correspondence and harmony among our feelings, thoughts, and actions. A morality flowing with the streams of emotional excitement is a morality subject to secret selfish desires, to errors of all kinds, and to exhaustion. A morality directed by reason is subject to the furnace of doubts, to hesitation, and to despair or cynicism. A morality of activism, of constant busy-ness, may conceal true inner needs and ignore criticism and reflection. All moral styles and attitudes are prone to becoming semiconscious habits, resulting in dead, empty, and cold moral attitudes and customs. Meditation, in which we quietly confront our feelings, our thoughts, and the results of our actions, tends to set them all in perspective with each other, adjust them to each other, and bring about a wholesome balance, in awareness and freedom. Better than any other moral method, meditation creates a moral symmetry and wholeness, so that in moral situations our whole self—body, breathing, heart, and mind—is thrown into right decisions. It is better to do the good with our whole being, and meditation makes this possible.

It is better, also, to love God with our whole being. Too many religious people withhold a good portion of themselves, turning their backs on the divine even as they pray with feeling, read scripture thoughtfully, or run around working "for the Lord." They hold back some portion of themselves and cheat God, often without knowing it and often with the encouragement of friends or family. For many it has become a habit to think and talk much about and with God, but with little feeling and fewer results in action. Getting down on our knees, while it does suggest an un-American posture of submission to a king, makes good sense from a meditation point of view, in that changes in body posture trigger a break from our habitual selves. Through meditation thinking Christians can become more than "Christians in thought." Feeling Christians, too, could do with a dose of meditation, to deepen and clarify religious feelings, to examine those feelings quietly, and to leave room for God's "feelings" to enter. Those whose love for God finds expression in action, in working for justice or to relieve suffering, must also avoid hiding themselves in their actions. We can become so one-sided and so noisy as we feel, think, or act out our religious style that we never pull ourselves together, sit quietly, and listen for the inner promptings of the spirit and of our own deeper, wider reality.

We can only hope that religious people and communities, who seem nowadays to be consumed by their zeal or by their doubt, would learn to meditate, alone or in small groups, preferably in churches and synagogues. Churches and synagogues are excellent meditation environments, and those who meditate in them will quickly break the habitual, sleepy attitude they have toward such places. If meditation groups do form in the religious places and groups of America, a wholesome, new, powerful, peaceful, and loving generation of Americans will emerge, to work toward the good, to express the beauty of human fulfillment, and to seek the truth which will make America free of fear, confusion, human and environmental decay, hatred, and "principalities and powers." But the time is short. Unless a significant number of well-prepared Americans can begin to practice and demonstrate a depth and fulfillment of self through peace-filled awareness and everyday actions, in concert with others, America will continue its pursuit of materialistic consumption, plastic individualism, social explosion, and moral homelessness ... until the end.

A TRAINING PROGRAM
IN MEDITATION

Introduction to the Training Program

The training program in meditation set forth in the following pages consists of a learning process that begins with elementary exercises in relaxation and concentration, proceeds to more advanced exercises such as walking meditation and meditation with words, focuses in on exercises useful in everyday life, including interpersonal meditation, and concludes with an experimental project of the meditator's own design. Upon completion of the training program, the meditator should be able to meditate effortlessly in a variety of everyday environments and situations, should possess a repertoire of exercises to apply to life and to develop experimentally, and should have reached the plateau where meditation is sufficiently mastered to become a life-long resource.

The program and the exercises reflect the concepts and concerns expressed in the first chapters of this book. They have been tested over a nine-year period and are an innovative blend of traditional exercises from the world's meditation traditions. The exercises, individually and in their progressive, cumulative effect, are designed to be done with the resources at hand for the average American, to be of practical use, and to benefit the meditator and others.

The exercises are described in a progressive order. That is, the meditator should gain confidence and experience in the first exercise before advancing to the second, should explore meditation with words before attempting interpersonal meditation. The pace of advance through the exercises is determined by several factors, but the full program should take no less than seven weeks. For those able to move rapidly and steadily through the program, it is suggested that they use the schedule of exercises included in the Appendix, "A Five-Week Program," adding two weeks to this schedule for their experimental project in everyday meditation. The seven-week schedule has been used successfully many times in a group situation or college course format where limits of time and the need to coordinate individual efforts make scheduling imperative as well as somewhat artificial. There are advantages to meditating in groups that outweigh the imposition of a schedule upon what is a prolonged growth process of individuals. Group meditation can maximize each meditation session's success for the individual because the group tends to share experience and insights, to require regular commitment to the practice, and to generate a shared and common feeling of acceptance and joint effort. If group meditation can be arranged, a rotating leadership system should be used, with each session's leader taking responsibility for signalling the beginning and end of the meditation exercise, perhaps by using a small bell. If meditation is used by a group that also plans to talk or work together, the meditation exercise should come before the discussion or action.

Most of us cannot make suitable arrangements to move rapidly and steadily through the training program or to develop our meditation practice in a group of meditators who share time and reserve space for the joint effort. With quiet dedication and self-discipline we must advance alone, one by one. Moving from exercise to exercise carefully and surely, accepting setbacks and interruptions, advancing at our own good pace, our meditation practice can gradually unfold through time. Some have taken as long as a year to introduce themselves to the full range of exercises in this training program.

To enhance the regularity of practice and to encourage calm observation of oneself through the training period, a meditation logbook can be used. Carefully and clearly enter into the logbook a description of your experience following each meditation period. Do not make the logbook a chore, a diary of self-analysis, or a checklist of exercises to be gotten out of the way. Do make it a record of your impressions of each session's success or weakness and of the conditions that influenced your meditation. Some entries will be brief, others will be long, as in the following examples from meditators' logbooks after they had completed one of the beginning exercises.

Day 1—Wednesday evening, September 1, 1976—bedroom.

EXERCISE: *Sitting meditation, eyes closed, counting the breath cycle.*

OBSERVATION: *After having assumed my position in the chair, I began counting, slowly, as I inhaled, and within minutes my eyelids began to get heavy, I was yawning quite a bit, and my head began to nod. It became increasingly hard to maintain counting, and the steady whir of the fan lulled me until the next thing I knew I was awakening with a start as my head gave a sudden jerk. I was too tired.*

*　　*　　*　　*　　*

Day 1—Wednesday evening, January 12, 1977—dorm room.

OBSERVATION: *This has made me feel very sleepy. I had much more trouble maintaining my concentration than earlier today. While I never lost my count, or went too high, I often had small internal discussions going on in addition to the counting. However, I was not aware at any time of external distractions. Again, I had to take a couple of larger breaths, which broke my rhythm, because the deep-belly breathing didn't seem satisfying. More time passed than I realized. I stopped because of a severe cramp, and saw that over fifteen minutes had passed (I had expected more like five). Why does time pass so quickly during meditation? For periods I was aware of nothing but the movement of my breathing, but at one point I noticed my torso rocking slightly with the breath. I guess I wasn't relaxed enough.*

Some entries in your logbook may record the inevitable sessions of trouble, confusion, or dryness that will occur. The following entry, for example, recorded the reaction of a meditator who was partially shocked by a loud interruption during a deeply inward, closed-eye meditation. It was to protect against such reactions that ancient Hindu social codes prescribed severe penalties against interrupting yogis and that meditators have preferred to practice in the protected isolation of monasteries. If the meditator making this entry had followed the program more carefully, particularly by meditating with her eyes open or partially open, she would not have been so shocked. In a sense, she diverted from the path of the program, a path that takes into account that deeply inward meditation is risky.

Day 19—Wednesday evening, September 15, 1976—dorm room.

EXERCISE: *Sitting meditation, meditating on the koan, mu.*
OBSERVATION: *I was really getting into it tonight—I felt almost as if I were floating, and yet I had no real feelings of isolation, as if I were the only one in the dorm, and very much solitary. Suddenly my girlfriend burst into the room announcing she had just gotten a call from this guy she's in love with, and suddenly it was as if someone had shattered a huge plate of glass. There was a sound within my mind that was very much like glass shattering, and for a split second everything went blank. It was hard for me to focus on things, and she, after realizing she had upset me, left the room. It was the strangest feeling, and I was not even able to do light reading after that. I ended up going to bed, and even then it took me almost an hour and a half to fall asleep. I just kind of lay there in a stupor.*

The feeling of strangeness lasted for the next twenty-four hours, a period of disorganization and disorientation for the meditator. Two weeks later, a similar interruption occurred, but her observation revealed a capacity to "roll with the punch," to absorb instantly outside interruptions without being jolted off-center by them:

I was really getting into it this morning and then my suitemate barged in the room—wow—it startled me—but oddly enough, not as much as the first time someone interrupted me. I seemed to be able to let it pass through me and still focus on my center.

Depending on the individual, the quality of her meditation, and the length of her practice, such interruptions can be mastered by depth of relaxation and firmness of concentration and alertness. If a meditator sits with a proper degree of openness or open-eyed alertness to the external environment, perhaps assisted by a vow not to allow the mind to be shaken even if the roof falls, most interruptions are transformed into simple events, neither pleasant nor unpleasant, just happenings.

At other times, logbook entries will record feelings and experiences of intense illumination, pleasure, and amazement, as the meditator begins to see with "new eyes." The following entry reports a not uncommon break through in meditation, in this case occurring while doing walking meditation on a trip downtown, through the slush, noise, and wind of a February afternoon.

Day 22—Friday afternoon, February 4, 1977—walking along Broadway.

EXERCISE: *Walking meditation.*

OBSERVATION: *At first it seemed pretty hopeless. Even though I kept concentrating on my breathing, a lot of thoughts kept zapping around in my head. After awhile I settled down, though, and got that queer feeling of distortion which I've taken to mean that I'm centered. I felt very elated and calm. I sort of felt high: Everything was very vivid, sharp smells, clear sounds, etc. But what hit me was how beautiful everything was! Even the lumps in the cement and the patterns of coal in the snow. I just had to laugh, I felt so good. I wonder sometimes if I'm crazy to get so much joy out of feeling in harmony with the world, instead of so alienated.*

Such experiences are gratifying and pleasant to beginning meditators, but if they become the goal of meditation, the meditation will falter when pleasant sensations do not arise, or become distorted into a method of pleasure-seeking. Such delights as do come through meditation should be accepted as gifts and as signs of progress; the same attitude should be taken up when less delightful happenings arise, for they will.

You are about to embark on an experimental journey into meditation. Prepare yourself by taking the following steps:

1. Relax.
2. Calmly reflect on your reasons for trying meditation and

what led *you* at *this time* to learn to do it. Write your reflections down.

3. Read or reread Chapters 2 and 3, "The Practice of Meditation" and "The Meditation Environment."

4. Tell your family and friends that you will be meditating twice a day for twenty-minute periods and that you would appreciate their support.

5. Decide on a place where you can do sitting meditation without interruption by other people for twenty minutes, and without disturbance by sharp sounds (like telephones).

6. Prepare a "meditation outfit" of loose-fitting, comfortable clothes. It is especially important to have a loose fit around your waist (no belt or girdle).

7. Select two times a day to be set aside for meditation. Do not meditate just before going to sleep or just after eating.

Once meditation begins and through the days of your learning and practice, problems will arise. Most problems in meditation can be dissolved by willing to persist in the practice and by adopting the attitude that minor doubts, failures, pains, and cramps are simply part of the process of unlearning old habits and learning new ways of physical, emotional, mental, and moral mastery. Feet falling asleep, an increase or decrease in normal dreaming patterns, feelings of euphoria or surplus energy, a sense of pride in what one is doing, and the "blues" when the meditation does not work—all these are normal experiences. The important thing, the focus of great concern, is to enter, practice, and cease each exercise period with a relaxed mind and body, to do each exercise as effortlessly as you can. Keep awake. Keep calm. Keep on meditating.

At the end of the training program, you will have learned to grasp several tools of the meditation process. You will have gained many insights into yourself and lost the hardness of your old habits. You will become a friend to yourself, a stronger and more gentle person for others, a child of this earth, a solution to the question of America, and more. You will have entered the stream, learned to swim, and begun the lifelong journey on the ebbing and flowing tides that will take you to the far shore of your being, to that which is the Being of us all.

The Fundamentals: Relaxation and Concentration

All meditation begins with exercises designed to reduce tensions of the body, breathing, and mind and to focus or concentrate the mental awareness of the meditator. Correspondingly, the exercises reveal the areas and degrees of tension and mental distraction that we habitually carry around. Finally, these exercises can serve as a fallback position, to retreat to when meditation becomes confusing, difficult, or filled with tensions of its own. That is, when meditation later produces problems, the meditator is wise to return to these basic exercises to determine where the tensions of life have lodged in the self and to rebuild the relaxed awareness that sometimes goes astray in advanced meditation.

In these exercises, the meditator will first learn how to completely relax and what relaxation feels like. Then he will proceed to a simple concentration or focusing exercise and link his focusing to relaxation through the process of centering, of focusing energy and awareness in his physical center or belly. On the foundation of these exercises, advanced techniques will then be erected securely, leading to a flexible and creative meditation style of life.

The reader is reminded that each meditation period should be fifteen to twenty minutes long. This is long enough to establish the exercise and to learn its tone or groove, but not so long as to let one fall asleep or move too deeply into meditation's more risky domain. Keeping to the daily schedule of two meditation periods, the meditator will quickly progress to the point of knowing what deep relaxation can be and how to focus his energies without wasting them.

Basic Relaxation Exercise

This exercise can be used at any time in one's life that tensions seem to be disruptive or destructive of physical health or mental balance. As a beginning exercise, however, it teaches and reveals the comprehensive relaxation that should be sustained in all other meditation exercises.

In a dimly lighted and quiet room, lie down on your back on a rug on the floor. Close your eyes and, under your eyelids, look without straining at the tip of your nose. Send inner messages to all parts of your body to relax or flop loosely, starting with your toes and feet, working up your legs to your stomach and chest. Then, send messages to fingers, hands, and arms to relax. Place your hands on your rising and falling stomach, placing the right hand on your navel and your left hand on top of the right. Relax your facial, neck, shoulder, and back muscles, especially the small or arch of your back. Tension usually finds a final refuge in facial muscles or in the small of the back.

As you breath in and out, imagine that tensions are flowing out and away through your exhalations, and that pure, gentle energy is slowly flowing into you through each inhalation. Imagine this process as if it were the ebb and flow of ocean tides. As you become more relaxed and more free of tensions, avoid the tendency to fall asleep or daydream. Allowing your breathing to cycle naturally, begin to count your breathes. Inhalation—*one*, exhalation—*two*, inhalation—*three*, and so on up to *ten*. At *ten* return to *one* again, and continue counting in cycles of ten. Returning to *one* you will avoid falling asleep. If you lose count or your attention wanders, return to *one* and begin counting again.

After fifteen minutes, stop counting and remain quietly breathing, focusing on the rise and fall of your stomach. When you feel peacefully relaxed raise your hands and arms above your body in a stretching, awakening gesture. Take a deep yawn and slowly rise to a sitting, then a standing, position. This will end the exercise. You should be able to observe several interesting things about what happens during and after this exercise. The major lesson to be learned in this exercise is finding and recognizing that point where relaxation is balanced with alertness. If you become too deeply relaxed and lose your alertness, you will fall asleep or rise from the exercise somewhat drowsy. If done correctly, the exercise at completion will cause you to rise with a sense of energy and renewal and with sharpened senses.

Basic Sitting Meditation Exercise

This exercise is an introduction to the basic process of doing meditation in a sitting position. The sitting position is the classic meditation position for good reasons. It is a relaxing position, but one that does not produce drowsiness as readily as a lying-down position does. A fruitful balance between relaxation and alertness can be achieved and held for long periods of time in sitting positions which are stable, firm, and without strain. The training program will rely upon the benefits of the sitting position in that at least one meditation session each day shall be in the sitting position.

In a dimly lighted and quiet room, sit on a straight-backed chair (like a kitchen or desk chair) so that your feet are flat on the floor. Sit forward on the chair seat so that your back does not rest on the chair back. Tilt slightly forward from the waist, letting your stomach muscles push forward so you feel that you have a "pot belly" and that your back is slightly arched. Place your right hand in your lap, palm up, and your left hand in or on the right hand. Alternatively, rest your hands on your thighs, palms upward, or fold your hands and place them in your lap. Choose the hand position that allows your shoulders to drop comfortably.

If you experience strain and stress in this sitting position, try to stretch your muscles by gently pressing or exaggerating the position, in order to overcome old posture habits based on sitting in soft, reclining chairs. Also check to see that your clothing is not tight around your waist or pulling at the knees.

Your head should be comfortably erect, with your chin tucked in slightly and your jaw set by lightly joining the teeth. If you wear eyeglasses most of the time, continue to wear them. If you wear contact lenses, they should be removed.

Closing your eyes as in the basic relaxation exercise, begin to count your breaths. The first few days you will count up to *ten* as in the relaxation exercise, but this will be simplified as soon as possible to counting only on exhalations.

As you count your breaths, focus your mind's eye on your belly area, sensing the push and pull, rise and fall of your stomach area as you breath in and out. Let your awareness sink down toward your belly more and more with each breath cycle. You should feel more and more relaxed with each breath cycle, at first as if you are falling asleep. Before becoming too drowsy and too inward, begin to imagine that your belly area is like a lighthouse, pulsing brighter and duller as you breath in (stomach pushing forward, light on; stomach contracting, light dims). Sustain the counting and the bright-dim cycle as the focus of your mind and your sensation of yourself.

Let your breath flow as it will, without trying to regulate or control it. Sometimes your breath cycle will seem uneven, too fast or too slow. Let your breath go by itself.

When thoughts or feelings or sensations enter awareness, in the spaces between the numbers, do not be disturbed by this ordinary occurrence. Just let them happen and return, without strain, to counting numbers and sensing the brightening and dimming of the lighthouse in your stomach area.

After fifteen or twenty minutes cease counting and remain sitting for one or two minutes. As you sit these couple of minutes, open your eyes and remain focused on the sensation of your stomach pushing out and collapsing with the breath cycle. Slowly rise from the chair and walk about or stand still while continuing to focus on your stomach motion for another minute or two. Take a deep yawn, stretch your arms over your head. This will end the exercise.

This exercise introduces the feeling of sitting meditation. The major lesson is to feel the stomach and breath cycle as the focus of awareness until you are able to sit and feel that your breath-stomach cycle is the center of your physical and mental awareness. You should be able to feel that your body, breathing, and mind are located or rooted in your stomach area, so that your sense of yourself is located more in your stomach (more precisely, about two knuckles-width below your navel) and less in your eyes, head, throat, or chest. If done correctly, the exercise will cause you to feel more balanced physically as you stand up, in that your mental center will be located more strongly in your physical center of gravity. If the exercise is done incorrectly, and you do not focus enough down in your stomach or are not relaxed enough, you will feel drowsy or tense at the end, perhaps with a slight headache.

At the end of this unit of practicing the fundamentals, you will have learned what the phrase *relaxed awareness* refers to in terms of body, breathing, and brain activity. You may also find yourself getting a little bored with the counting focus; if so, you must muster your will power (without getting tense) and continue counting, for counting builds your strength as a concentrator who can focus. Most importantly, however, try to relax into your stomach center and enjoy it.

Open-Eye Meditation: Centering and Walking Meditation

While the first unit consisted of learning the basic meditation attitude, common to all meditation traditions and teaching, the second unit's exercises mark a turning point in meditation, moving the meditator in a direction different from most classical paths. Usually meditation proceeds quietly and progressively into a deep inward probing of the unconscious, in detachment from the world, from daily life, from the senses, or even from the body. Locked in inward adventure, the meditator seeks an illumination, a radical transformation of self, at the bottom of consciousness. This is the way of the traditional mystic, of trance, of "dark nights of the soul," of cosmic consciousness, of ecstacy. But the way of this book is different, aiming at a meditation of everyday life as it is lived by most Americans. The heroism of the mystic, supported and protected by wise teachers and strong, specialized religious communities, is rare, difficult, and dangerous. We aim in a different direction, to an American setting lacking in wise teachers and energetic mystical communities, toward the goal of transforming everyday American life through the efforts of ordinary people, who are not "heroic," who ought not risk the dangers of meditation that goes to the abyss, but who, nevertheless, possess the faith, will, and insight to practice a meditation path of consequence to themselves and to the shape and meaning of America.

Having tasted the feeling of meditation in the first exercises —a feeling of inward rest, control, and stability—the meditator is now asked to shift the focus of effort and awareness away from the inner sense of body, breathing, and mind *to the degree necessary to connect his inner awareness with the external and everyday world.* Not giving up a keen and balanced inner center of relaxed awareness, the meditator literally and figuratively opens his eyes in meditation to re-establish interaction and awareness of the world outside his body, breathing, and mind, in order to sense the body, breathing, and mind of the world. This turn around of awareness is to be made for three reasons. First, by not losing connection with the external environment during meditation sessions, the meditator greatly reduces the psychological distortions and manifestations (such as hallucinations, euphoria, or apathy) that usually emerge after awhile in deeply inward, closed-eye meditation practices. They may still occur in open-eye meditation, but less frequently and with only slight effect. They should be viewed, if they occur, as signs that you are too inward or too sleepy in your meditation. Whether they are pleasant or unpleasant, dismiss these special events as the children of your desires and fears, which they are. By centering awareness in your meditation center, your belly, you will cause these and other symptoms to fade and disappear.

A second reason for the shift to open-eye meditation emerges from the fact that this is a meditation involved in everyday life. Unless your eyes are open, literally, you will not be able to move about very well in the real world of driving cars, cooking dinner, working with others, and crossing streets. An open-eye meditation makes it possible to perform these tasks with a meditation attitude, to act in the world effectively at the same time that you are centered in stillness. The third reason for open-eye meditation as the path of choice is that it discloses a subtle truth, forgotten as much by modern, secular people as by some inward, immobile mystics: that the distinction between inner and outer realities is probably false, and certainly misleading. The inner, private world of the mystic and of the ego-oriented executive or scholar is based on a forgetfulness that our bodies, breathing, and minds are networks tied into and dependent on the networks of the world's "body," flows and rhythms, and patterns of idea and sentiment. An open-eye meditation confirms the ecological theory that all things and events are intertwined and interactive with each other, continuously and absolutely, and reveals that we can be secure and free in interrelationships. Further, open-eye meditation can bring us to the point where we see the outside world *as it is*, unclouded by desire or fear and free of habitual or conceptual distortion. This path of meditation makes it possible to sense and know the world and others clearly, calmly, and with vivid freshness.

During this second unit, the meditator will first learn modifications in sitting meditation. Some modifications simply perfect the sitting position so that it becomes more stable physically, but most modifications are aimed to produce the open-eye attitude in sitting that will be used as the primary meditation exercise through the remaining weeks of the training program. This primary meditation exercise of open-eyed sitting meditation or centering should be practiced once a day from the beginning of the second unit. (Often the centering posture is used as the basis of various other exercises introduced as one progresses.) In this unit the student will also learn walking meditation, the exercises by which meditation can be sustained while moving, walking, or even running through the day. Walking meditation is the opening experience to a meditation style that finds opportunity for practice in ordinary situations of everyday life.

Centering Exercise: Open-Eye Sitting Meditation

The word *zazen* comes from the Japanese tradition of Zen Buddhism and literally means sitting meditation (*za*—seat or chair; *zen*—meditation). Zazen is practiced with eyes open, in contrast to the closed-eye meditation of Hindu yoga. The centering exercise described below is like, but not identical to, the formal zazen practiced by Japanese laity and monks.

The centering exercise may be viewed as a modification of the basic sitting meditation exercise introduced in the first unit. The centering exercise includes specific modifications in sitting posture, eye posture, breathing, and mental focus. Nevertheless, as you try out each of these modifications, seek out the feeling of relaxed awareness and centering in your belly that you discovered and repeated during the first unit. Do not be satisfied with a modification until you can do it in relaxed awareness. For example, when you open your eyes in meditation, it will seem very different from closed-eye meditation until and unless you remain relaxed, aware, and, especially, centered and comfortably balanced.

The centering exercise is a twenty-minute exercise, but the

sitting posture used can be comfortably sustained for thirty minutes or more. The sitting posture you must now learn (unless a physical handicap prevents your sitting in this fashion) is known as the half-lotus position. Sit on the floor in a cross-legged fashion. Place a firm cushion two to six inches in height under your bottom, which will raise your trunk and lower your knees. Sit *forward* on the cushion so that your trunk tilts forward slightly and your knees descend almost to the floor. It is like sitting half on and half off the cushion. Now place one foot in such a way that its heel is tucked in toward your crotch and touching the pillow below your crotch. With your hands place the other foot in the notch between calf and thigh, in such a way that the bottom of the foot is slightly upward. Better yet, try to place this foot on top of the thigh, if you can stretch everything. The bottom of the foot should then be facing upward, and the top of the foot should be in your thigh, close to the notch of your thigh and your trunk. Experiment, finding the foot position that is most comfortable for the period of time that you meditate.

Do not worry if your foot falls asleep, this is not unusual. There is some stretching and practice required before your foot will feel comfortable near or on your thigh. After squirming and adjusting, you should find this sitting position stable and comfortable. Your trunk will feel elevated and look dignified. Remember to tilt forward at the waist so your stomach drops toward your lap and is freed for relaxed stomach breathing. Remember to loosen any belt or restriction around your waist, and to keep pants loose around the bend in your knees (pull your pants up three or four inches before bending your knees).

After placing your hands together in your lap area and relaxing your shoulders, take two or three deep breaths, inhaling slowly and fully and exhaling slowly and completely. Closing your eyes, let your breath find its normal rhythm and begin counting on exhalations on the one–ten cycle.

When you feel relaxed and concentrated after five or ten minutes of closed-eye meditation, gently open your eyes. With your head erect and chin tucked in slightly, your eyes should be looking at an area three to six feet in front of you on the floor. Maintain this open-eyed position until the end of your meditation. Your eyes will probably be partially closed, and soon you will "see" the area in front of you but not have the sense of "looking at" it. Visually, it should feel as if you have a vague, general awareness of the area in front and toward the sides, but you are not focusing on anything in the area. This open-eyed position will lessen the tendency to become too drowsy and inward in meditation and, therefore, will lessen the risk of being shocked by a sudden sound or other stimulus from outside. Further, this eye position will prove useful in developing a meditation style and exercises for meditating during everyday activities.

The first few times of open-eyed meditation, continue counting the one–ten cycle while your eyes are open. But as soon as you feel comfortable with eyes open in meditation, drop the counting focus altogether. When you are no longer counting, focus instead on your center, using the sensation of your stomach muscles moving as the focus. Try to go beyond even this minimal focus, however, by focusing with all your mind and energy on the *fact and process of sitting itself.* Become SITTING: If an idea flashes across your awareness, the idea has risen from SITTING. Do not lose awareness that the only reality is SITTING. If your mind wanders or you become drowsy, try one of several gimmicks to center and awaken your awareness. Your mind should be as alert as you can make it, and resting in your relaxed SITTING. One gimmick is to imagine yourself to be sitting in an electric chair, composed and ready to die. Another is to imagine that your mind is resting in the palm of your left hand. Another is to feel imaginatively the effect of cold water pouring down on you from a waterfall or shower as you sit beneath it. Sometimes you can blink your eyes several times to overcome the drowsiness of the centering posture, of SITTING and DOING NOTHING. Remember, sit with all the energy you have.

The centering exercise should become the heart of your training program and later meditation practice, and you should do it in one of your two meditation sessions each day. It will deepen and maintain your ability to do other meditation exercises and should serve as a reference point for what centering, relaxation, and awareness mean.

Walking Meditation Exercise

Meditation in the walking posture may seem odd at first thought, given the prestige and emphasis of sitting meditation in most traditions. Nevertheless, there are instances of meditation in walking and strolling in meditation history. In some cases walking is used as a brief exercise interlude between long periods of sitting meditation. The purposes of walking meditation in this training program, however, center on the belief that a morally effective meditation is one that can be practiced in all situations. By learning and practicing meditation while you walk, you will discover that meditation is not something you do only when you can find the leisure to sit off in the corner, but something you can do while moving about in the center of your room; it is an attitude to be practiced, exercised, and put to work in any situation of life. Furthermore, walking meditation returns you to feeling your bodily life, a feeling that is reduced to breathing awareness in sitting meditation. Just as the body is the quiet root of meditation in the sitting position, so can it become the graceful base and testimony to meditation in action. The perfection of meditation in movement might be seen in the composure, balance, grace, and quickness of masters of some of the martial arts, who have gone beyond the violence of their judo, karate, or aikido into a realm of quiet and selflessness that makes of their movements an art form and perhaps more.

Your first attempt at walking meditation should immediately follow a session of the centering exercise. After sitting, rise as soon as you can to your feet, trying to retain the relaxation, awareness, and centering you achieved in sitting. Stand for a few minutes, with eyes directed at the floor about six to eight feet in front of you, feet placed at a little less than shoulder width, and with your hands placed gently on your chest so that your right hand is in a light fist and your left hand is covering your fist. Your elbows should be elevated and to the sides, your shoulders relaxed. In this standing position, focus on your stomach-breathing process, trying to feel yourself into this physical center of gravity so that you feel balanced. When you feel balanced, relaxed, and alert, begin walking a circuit that you can easily maneuver in and through. You can make a circuit of a room several times, provided the room is large enough and free of obstructions. A hallway may also serve. You should be able to walk your circuit for ten minutes without interruption. Eventually, rather than a small circuit that you walk around several times, you can find regular long circuits (a meditation trail?) and even make every walking opportunity of five minutes or longer an opportunity for meditation.

Your walking pace may be very slow, a shuffle of one foot movement every two seconds, may be at a normal walking pace, or may break into a jog. The quickness of pace is something to mindfully experiment with, as if you are seeking your own natural and easy walking pace. The slower you walk, the more aware you become of each movement and of the tiny imbalances of your walking. In slow walking the tendency is to feel that your walk is jerky and that your self-center is in your head. In normal pace walking, the tendency is to lose awareness, and you sink into the comfortable rhythm of walking. In fast walking, you tend to be centered well and your breathing is quick and heavy, but you can lose your brightness and relaxation of awareness under the impact of your steps pounding away. Try walking both with and without shoes. When walking without shoes, you can avoid a jerkiness of step by placing the outside of the soles of your feet down first and letting the rest of the sole, heel, and toes follow in a curling effect.

As you walk, remain centered in your abdominal area. Walk from your hips, so to speak, and get out of your head. Let your breathing find its own level in relation to the effort of walking slow or fast. Walk with dignity, balance, suppleness, fullness, and gentleness.

In these times of the automobile and of serious endeavor, we have lost to some degree the feeling and knowledge of walking for its own sake. Often we walk only as a means of getting from one place or purpose to another, our awareness wandering or focused on our destination or point of departure. In meditation walking, we focus on walking itself. As you center your awareness in your belly, let that awareness flow from your belly center into your whole body, breathing, and brain, so that you feel that you are totally involved in walking, in expressing walking, in *being* WALKING. Rather than reserve a part of your self-consciousness ("Here I am, doing walking meditation"), throw all your consciousness into your center and from there into JUST WALKING.

Sometimes JUST WALKING does not work as a focus. You might then try to achieve the ease, balance, and centering of proper walking meditation by doing a panther walk. Imagine that you are being taught to walk by imitating the mountain lion that is your teacher and companion while you walk along. After you get the hang of walking like the mountain lion, imagine that you are the mother of a cub, trying to show it how to walk like a mountain lion should walk as you walk along together, pacing, prowling, padding through space. At the end of your panther walk, you might try sitting meditation, with your panther lying beside you.

When walking is at a normal pace, we tend to fall sleepily into the rhythm and habit of walking. To wake up your walking, you might image you are walking toward your death (in a sense, you are) and that you will do it as wide awake as possible. To check whether your walking is balanced and flexible, imagine that you might have to leap, during any phase of your step, to avoid a falling bucket of paint, a crack in the ground, or a sudden attack from the rear.

Walking meditation should last for ten to twenty minutes. At the end of a session of walking, stand in position for a moment or two, let your arms fall to your side, and then go about your business. You may also drop your arms from the upright position during the last minute or two or walking, allowing them to swing easily as you walk. This will allow you to compare meditation walking with normal walking and will prepare you for the day when all your walking is meditation walking, so that when you set out normally to walk, arms swinging as they will, you will be doing meditation walking for yourself but it will appear quite normal to casual observers. We could call this secret meditation walking, but then we might get "puffed up" about the secretiveness of our walking.

The walking meditation exercise should be something done for the purpose of training ourselves to find and sustain the meditation attitude while our bodies are in motion. It can be done, in the arms swinging position of normal walking, several times a day. Walking meditation is, finally, a corrective to the one-sidedness of sitting meditation, a meditation resource when we are too nervous or active to sit, and a healthy exercise to build the physical strength and tone needed for sitting meditation.

Meditation with Words: From Silence to Prayer

During the second unit of meditation, you were asked to meditate from your center in such a way that your awareness would be focused on expressing nothing but SITTING, or SITTING IN AWARENESS, or WALKING. In such exercises your whole effort of body, breathing, and mind was directed to feeling and being what is portrayed by those words such that you were able to become WALKING or SITTING without reserve or hesitation. As you meditated SITTING, no doubt you formed an image of sitting that you tried to make real. You may also have said to yourself, as you tried to focus on SITTING, "sitting." That is, you used a word to focus your mind and will, to remind you of what you were about, and, perhaps, to block out other words that came into your mind as you SAT. If you used words in this way, you were close to the traditional use of words in meditation.

Probably most traditional meditation is focused and supported by the use of words during the meditation process at one stage or another. Seldom are the words of meditation used in a discursive or "thinking" way, as when we speak, read, write, or listen for the meaning of the words. Rather, words are used, ironically, to block out discursive thinking and to achieve a focus on one point. Contrary to ordinary usage, the word *meditation* does not mean to think, but to "no-think," to cease the conceptual, verbal habits that make our minds such useful tools for making sense of the world.

The most common use of words in traditional meditation is found in what the Hindus call mantra, which can also denote a way of using words in meditation in other traditions. The Great Mantra of Hinduism (and perhaps of Buddhism, too) is the practice of intoning to oneself or chanting aloud the sound *om* or *aum*. A fascinating variety of meanings have become attached to *om*, but essentially it is used for its effects during meditation, as the sound that is uttered on exhalations of breath. *Om* is used to begin and end a prayer or a long mantric formula of many sound-words, but it can also be chanted alone, again and again, during the cycle of breathing. The sound of *om*, plus the concentration required to repeat it and to fill one's awareness with *om*, combine to establish the relaxed alertness that we call meditation. The same effect can be achieved by other sounds and words. Christians, particularly Christians of the Eastern Orthodox church, practice a mantra when they repeat the Jesus prayer, "Lord, our God, have Mercy," in the *hesychast* practice. Constant, attentive, and gentle repetition of a phrase, sometimes a phrase that makes no sense and has no meaning, produces the relaxation and concentration which are the foundation of meditation.

The effect of the mantra is to calm, focus, and fill our awareness. There is some evidence that almost any sound or word or phrase, when repeated with alertness (if not done with alertness, the repetition lulls us to sleep), will have the desired effect of producing a quiet mind. Saying *one*, on and with each exhalation, for example, can produce the same effects as saying *om*. The same intention and effort, to calm and control the mind, can be seen, perhaps, when Mary Poppins sings *Supercalifragilisticexpialidocious*, or when we merely "whistle while we work" or "whistle a happy tune." The meaning of what we whistle or intone as sound and word is of secondary, if any, importance in mantra practice. The mantra is a concentration and and relaxation device, although traditional meditation interpretations link the sound with cosmic vibrations, psychic energies, or the name of the Absolute.

Mantric practice tends to produce an inward-turning awareness, although it need not result in complete detachment from the external environment. Another way of using words in meditation, developed in Zen Buddhism in China and Japan, is radically inward in its goal. The *koans* of Zen are intellectual puzzles that cannot be solved by reason, but only resolved or dissolved by a deep intuitive breakthrough into the unconscious levels of the self. Familiar koans are "What is the sound of one hand clapping?" or, in answer to a monk's question "Can a dog be a Buddha?" the koan of "No, nothingness," or "Mu" (*Mu* means nothing, no, nothingness). Usually, some essential phrase such as *one hand* or *mu*, becomes a mantra-like focus in koan practice, the meditator focusing on one hand throughout the days until a sudden breakthrough into the deepest self, beyond the ego and habitual self, happens. The

depth of breakthrough is measured by a master, who can de-
tect the energy, sincerity, and success with which the koan
meditator has attacked or "been attacked by" the koan.

Some modern Zen masters have said that a koan is any
existential or life-and-death question, phrase, or word that
emerges from our experience, such as "Who am I?" or "What
should I do the rest of my life?" If these or other questions
emerge, not as abstract or idle words, but as words that gnaw
at us, that we *must* answer somehow or die, we are facing a
koan. Unlike the mantra, the koan has meaning; but like the
mantra, the koan works on a level or in a way such that reason
and habit cannot come to grips with it. One Zen teacher makes
this very clear by the way he answers questions like "What does
Buddhism say about world hunger" or "Did the Buddha believe and teach that there is no soul?" He always answers,
"Who is it that asks this question?" By this answer he seeks to
make the questioner aware of his or her immediate reality,
which is more important than an abstract question.

Koans, then, may be understood as questions, puzzles, or
words that involve us deeply, that keep us off balance, that can
be solved only be an experience of our deepest self and not by
reason alone or by reference to lofty but dead words. Koan
practice consists of meditating on such questions, doubts, and
mysteries, most often by intuitively selecting the key word in
the question and meditating with that word as the focus. If the
koan, "Who am I, *really,* through all time?" emerged, for example, it would be taken into meditation by a focus on the one
word that the meditator felt was the key to the whole phrase.
As you sat in meditation, you might repeat in your belly or
center the sound of *Who,* perhaps searching with all your body,
breathing, and mind for WHO is meditating. Answers in word
forms may arise or they may not, but the search for WHO will
lead you deep into meditation and into the broad and deep
dimensions of awareness, if *who* is a "true" word for you and
if you throw your energies into the search. So powerful is the

koan practice, however, that it includes serious psychological risks, including physical disorientation and, at the extreme, psychosis. It should not be practiced for more than a few days unless you are under the direction of a qualified Zen teacher. It should not be practiced if you are under great tension. Nevertheless, it can be a significant and fruitful exercise to meditate on your koans, that is, to face and probe your life questions in the stability, calm, and concentration of meditation.

A step further toward meaningful use of words in meditation brings us to prayer and speech. Normally, we think of prayer as communication, speaking to God in petitioning his blessings of understanding, mercy, and protection or in thanking him for blessings received. The Christian tradition has usually distinguished these prayers of address or speaking from the prayer of quiet or prayer of silence, which is also called contemplation and is virtually the same as meditation. Can we pray in the sense of speaking to God without having learned the way to *listen* to God and the Spirit?

Meditation can be joined to a life and practice of prayer in two ways. First, meditation can be developed to increase our ability to sit quietly, to compose ourselves, to detach ourselves from trivial concerns, and to clear our awareness before we petition or thank God in spoken prayer. Meditation can help us calm, focus, and center our whole selves, body, emotions, and mind before we open our mouth and hearts. Sadly, the usual practice in many American church worship services does not allow enough time, not to mention the training, for meditative composure before praying. Hymns are sung, business is transacted, one minute of silence comes, and then everyone launches into a mumbling of the Lord's Prayer, as if the mere mouthing of these words was effective for us and pleasing to God. Try saying the Lord's Prayer after twenty minutesof the centering exercise, however, and you will find a weight and awesomeness to the words that you may never have experienced before unless you have heard or said the words in a time of crisis.

Meditation can also be developed so that during prayer we can be praying meditatively, that is, with the intensity of our being. Saying the words, not with the mouth or head alone, but with our whole self centered, energetic, and focused, is possible and desirable. Meditation, as the training program makes clear, is an attitude for action as well as sitting, for social environments as well as lonely corners. It is also an attitude in which to speak as well as an attitude in which to listen to the sounds of silence. Based upon your experience with meditating in and from your belly center, try to pray silently, then aloud, so that the words and sounds issue from that place, rather than from your head or mouth. Praying from your meditation center, you will come to know what praying with all your heart, body, mind, and soul means. It means you are centered and focused on speaking and praying, not on yourself or saying the words correctly or keeping pace with the person leading the prayers. Of course, since you will not be praying in the habitual way, you may get carried away in praying, lose the pace, pray too loudly and too fully, and cause heads to turn. People will wonder, perhaps, why you pray so enthusiastically, with so much energy and enthusiasm. If you were not so immersed in praying, you would probably wonder why they pray so dully, solemnly, in a fashion they would never use if they were trying to really communicate. Many of us get in the habit of concealing ourselves in and during prayer, and would jump out of our skins if God answered immediately.

The word-sound exercises should be viewed as experimental, as exercises where you try to link sound, then words, and then meaning to your meditation practice and attitude. No mantra are secretly given to you in these exercises that you can pride yourself in hoarding. Try sounding the word *one* or the sound *Ohmmmmm.* See how they fit your breathing pattern, your feeling of the center, and your intuition. If they work, that is, if they relax you, help you to gently center yourself, and seem satisfying and complete to you, keep using them. Better yet, find your own sound, word, or even your own koan. If you know and are comfortable with prayers, you will benefit by meditating before and during prayer. It will become obvious to you, if you try to speak from your center, that this is both a refreshing and a difficult action. It is not easy to sustain a prayer or talking when you are centered and speaking from your center, that is, with your whole being.

Mantra Exercise

The repetition of and focus upon a sound, word, or phrase in the mantra exercise is performed to produce relaxation of body and mind and to bring the rush of mental events to a halt. Mantra meditation tends to take an inward path and block awareness of the external environment, so that even though mantra can be practiced while walking and in noisy environments, it is best to practice the mantra during sitting meditation in a place free from disturbance and noise.

The mantra exercise should be practiced as a dimension of the centering exercise. Assume the centering posture, being careful to sit comfortably alert and relaxed and to let your stomach muscles drop forward and down as you inhale. Taking two or three deep breathes, filling and emptying your lungs completely (start by expanding your stomach on the inhalation, letting your chest rise as you complete the inhalation, and end by pressing the air out completely on the exhalation using your stomach muscles). Close your eyes. With your breath following a normal rhythm, begin to silently and inwardly "sound" the mantra on your exhalations. Your inhalations are silent. As you sound the mantra, imagine it as falling from your throat into your belly, along the route of your spine, as you exhale. At the bottom of the exhalation, imagine the sound of the mantra as resting in your belly center, with each mantra that "drops" adding a bit more energy to the mantra that is building in your belly center, like layers of lacquer on a small egg. With each exhalation a mantra layer is added to the egg. This part of the mantra exercise should be deeply relaxing and inward.

After ten minutes of "layering the egg with mantras," open your eyes. Continue layering the egg for three or four breath cycles, then cease dropping mantras from your throat. Begin to imagine that the movement of your stomach muscles, pressing forward and collapsing in the breath cycle, is the breathing of your mantra, so that it is not you but the mantra that breathes, that expands and contracts its energy and vibrations. It is a feeling that you are being breathed and energized by the mantra egg in your belly center. Your breathing now should be slow, gentle, and easy.

At the end of twenty minutes bring your mantra exercise to a close by blinking your eyes, raising and stretching your arms and hands, unfolding your legs, and sitting quietly for a minute or two. You should feel deeply relaxed, and sometimes slightly euphoric or elevated, after this exercise.

After some experience with silently and inwardly sounding the mantra, you should try several times, until you get the hang of it, to sound the mantra aloud by humming quietly the mantra on the exhalation or by sounding it louder. This can be uncomfortable for some people because of the feeling that someone may hear them and think them odd. Our business-like, serious society has grown less tolerant and more ignorant of people making playful sounds in public, whether the sounds be children playing, people singing or humming, or young men and women whistling, while we seem strangely to be comforted by the whirr of machines, the whine of tires, or the drone of airplanes. Resist your society; chant aloud. If you are practicing in a congenial group of meditators, chant together, as you might sing or pray together, with boldness and harmony.

Koan Exercise

The koan exercise procedure is much like the mantra exercise, but instead of a mantra one meditates on a genuine, meaningful question after reducing the question to one key word. Perhaps there are koans of universal depth, effective for everyone at all times in opening to depths of insight on Great Puzzles. But for purposes of the training program the koans should be those existential questions that are buzzing around underneath the surface of everyday awareness, those puzzles or conflicts that are particularly yours right now. What do you hope for, inwardly? What is the major conflict within yourself, right now, or the conflict between you and others, right now?

Taking a pencil and paper, write down a speculative, spontaneous list of the questions you ask yourself in your private moments of victory or defeat, of boredom or contentment, of desire or depression. You might have a habit that you wish to strengthen or one you wish to eliminate. A moral dilemma might be the focus of your inquiry with yourself. After writing the list, review it, crossing out trivial questions and phrases, and underline the important phrases. Take one of the underlined items and clarify the words into a question, such as, "Why do I smoke?" "What should I do to end my depressed mood?" "What can I do best?" "What, finally, is me?" or "What is happening with John?" Find the key word in the question, as *John* might be the key word in the last example. This word becomes your meditation focus, your koan in essence.

If the question is a genuine one and important *to you*, you will already have given it some thought and invested some emotion and energy in it. By taking it into meditation, you are able to work on it as if from another angle. Adopt the centering posture. Start with your eyes closed only enough to gain relaxation, then open them and let the key word sound on your exhalation much as the mantra word does. As the word sinks to your belly center, let it disappear into the darkness. (Do not, as with a mantra, let the word layer an egg.) As you proceed, your feelings toward the word will shift and whirl. An image may appear of the word or of what the word refers to. Other words will emerge, some a new insight on the koan, some simply humorous. Just let the process flow, but return to the key word with each exhalation, letting the word fall with each exhalation into your belly and into nothingness.

Since the koan is so much connected with what we have thought with our minds, it often happens that as the word falls to the center, our heads become busy, thinking all kinds of things. This can be fascinating, even informative, but try to rest your mind in your center, and keep your awareness stable, at ease, and centered. End the koan exercise by ceasing to drop the key word and sitting silently in centering meditation for about two minutes with your focus only on the feeling of breathing in your stomach.

Stomach Strengthening Exercise

The deep stomach breathing of the centering posture tends to stretch and strengthen the muscles of the belly area. During centering your stomach extension will resemble a "pot" or fat belly. This is proper, but you may notice after two or three weeks of extending your stomach area forward to breathe freely that not only are your abdominal muscles becoming stronger, they are also more extended. You are developing a "meditation belly," like the round-bellied laughing Buddhas of China. The following exercise will counteract that tendency and even help flatten your abdomen.

Twice a day, go through the following routine, but not during meditation. You can do it while standing. Inhaling, pull in your stomach tightly (not too tightly), holding this sucked-in position for a count of six (about six seconds), then releasing it with an exhalation. Repeat the inhalation-contraction, followed by exhalation, ten times each time you do this exercise.

You will notice that with each contraction your buttocks will also tend to contract and be exercised. A strong bottom, of course, is not undesirable for meditators who do sitting meditation!

Environmental Meditation: Opening the Senses

Meditation practices that stress the use of mantra and koan, sometimes to the exclusion of other meditation methods, tend to develop over time as deeply inward, introspective, and detached meditation lifestyles. Furthermore, when the mantra practice revolves around a single mantra, the meditator tends to become habituated to and dependent upon the routine use of the mantra to gain the fruits of meditation; the meditation becomes more inflexible in terms of the meditator's ability to achieve the meditation state of centering in different situations; and the meditator may mistakenly begin to view the mantra as a magical technique, that is, as an automatic device by which to turn on meditation states without reflection, moral discipline, or sincerity. Mantra are useful in every meditation, but only if we appreciate their limited function as triggers of a more important reality, our many-sided self. Since the aim of meditation is the freeing and gentling of a human personality so that it might be more wise, deep, energetic, loving, and alive, meditators must recognize the need for many skillful means to achieve this goal. Just as there are many potential mantra for awakening and regulating an inner awareness, just as there are many koans or existential dilemmas erupting in us to bring about insight and personal decisions, so there are meditation approaches to awaken us to awareness and responsiveness in the external world of the environment and of other people.

In this unit, you will experiment with exercises designed to balance the inwardness of mantra and koan meditation with a capacity to respond intensely and clearly to the outer environment with your senses. The aim of these exercises is to connect the inwardness of meditation with the external environment through a discipline of the senses, a discipline in which we hear, see, taste, smell, and touch the world of things with our centers . . . and our centers become responsive to the world of things.

Through a meditation-centered discipline of the senses, Americans can become more sensitive to what is bombarding us through the senses as we move in and respond to everyday environments. Much of the sensory stimulation we receive is chaotic or "noisy"—often it is loud, seldom is it under our control, rarely is it satisfying. The sensed environment is inescapably wrapping us in sounds, sights, tastes, and aromas that are too often unpleasant. We escape the unpleasantness or interference of the sensed environment, not by changing the environment, but by screening it out, either with counter-stimulations (like deodorants or loud stereos) or with a habitual desensitizing of ourselves so that we do not notice what our senses are receiving and registering on our nervous systems. Our senses become narrowed, jaded, or closed down, and we lose contact with and enjoyment of the splendors of creation. Through a discipline of the senses, we learn to sense once again, to face the ugly facts of our artificially constructed sensed environment, and, perhaps, to make changes in that environment to restore its natural richness and rhythms. Meditation, aiming to awaken us, can also awaken our senses, the gateways to the world.

Traditional meditation, in seeking often a detached and inner reality, sought to close the gates of the senses as a means of opening the doors of inner consciousness. This training program, however, in seeking a balance of self between inner search and outer responsiveness to the American scene as well as moral responsibility, insists that meditation must be seen in America as a way of engagement with the world as well as with the self. The discipline of the senses is a way of training for awareness of the world, but it is also a way of checking that meditation is not becoming too inward. By knowing and practicing a meditation approach that remains always aware of the environment in which they are actually sitting or walking in meditation, meditators avoid the psychological risks of inward meditation and gain a flexible, responsible, everyday style of meditation.

This unit's exercises are two in kind and purpose. First, the meditator is encouraged to modify centering practice so that it becomes a way of meditating with open eyes and open senses. Centering in this way, in contrast to centering practiced with mantra or koan, can become a meditation of opening oneself more or less totally to the time and place in which one sits. One becomes aware that there are mantras all around in the silences and signals of the environment and that the most complete and free meditation is one that does not, finally, create a barrier or conflict between inner and outer reality, between self and world. To achieve this complete and open awareness a simple exercise is suggested—namely, to begin to meditate in an environment that is deliberately not as quiet and free of interruption as the environment suggested at the beginning of the training program.

Second, to discipline the senses, a series of exercises are described, each focusing on a different sense. Meditators should try to awaken each sense deliberately and to connect the sense with their center, the balancing point for all meditative awareness. By learning to open each sense, the meditator will turn meditation into the world of things and action and prepare the basis for interpersonal meditation, where meditation is turned into the world of people-awareness and moral sensitivity.

Thunder Exercise: Testing Exercise for Openness

This exercise should be used periodically in meditation practice to determine whether you are relaxed, alert, and open to the environment during meditation and in everyday life. It consists of deliberate interruptions of the quiet of meditation by sounds both pleasant and unpleasant and observation of yourself as you respond to the sudden sounds. If you are disturbed by the sounds, it means your meditation is too inward, that you have developed a habit of preferring a passive, self-involving awareness disconnected from the world, or that your meditation is more like becoming drowsy than coming awake, or that your meditation is filled with physical or mental tension. If the sounds flow through you without disturbing your calm centering, if you are fully aware of them but unshaken by them, your meditation is centered, deep, and open.

The thunder exercise consists of introducing certain sounds into the room in which you are practicing the centering exercise, of sitting with the focus of JUST SITTING, or a mantra or koan exercise (centering posture position). If you are meditating alone in your practice, you should make a tape recording of the sounds for playback while you sit in meditation. If you are meditating in a group, one member of the group should have the responsibility and the sound instruments to make the sounds for the entire group. Allowing five to eight minutes for meditation to become relaxed and stabilized, introduce the following sounds into the environment, in the order given, at a moderate volume level. First, using a small bell or music triangle with a delicate and pleasant sound, make a soft ringing sound, repeating the sound about every five seconds for a period of thirty seconds. Wait about three minutes, then, using a drum like a tom-tom (not a snare drum with its sharp sound), an empty kleenex box and spoon, a hollow wooden clacker, or any instrument that makes a hollow, neutral, neither pleasant nor unpleasant sound, make a thudding, hollow sound, repeating the sound every five seconds or so for a period of thirty seconds. Finally, after another three minutes, using two blocks of wood crashing against each other, make a sharp, irritating, unpleasant, and loud sound every five seconds or so for a period of thirty seconds.

If you are tense, drowsy, off-center, or too inward in your sitting meditation, these sounds will disturb your meditation, in the sense of interrupting it as if from a place outside yourself. If you are open, stable, and well-centered, these sounds will appear clearly, as if they are very close to you, almost inside you, and will not surprise you. The sounds will simply appear and disappear, as if they briefly passed into and through you. You may be "electrified" or stimulated by the sounds, but that is a normal and positive reaction. If you are shocked and disoriented by the sounds, your meditation is not centered, relaxed, alert, or open. It needs correction if you are pursuing this training program.

The lesson of the thunder exercise is that the awareness of the meditator must be flexible, responsive, and alert as well as relaxed, stable, and centered. Sometimes in everyday life the world will arrange to produce its own thunder exercise for you, as when a sonic boom or auto backfire or crash of thunder breaks into your awareness and, through your response, reveals to you whether you are becoming too oblivious to your environment, too tense, or too sleepy—or whether you are centered.

Sense Training Exercises: Opening the Gates of the Senses

This series of sense training exercises is designed to awaken and sharpen each of the five senses and to connect each sense to your belly center of awareness. You may already have noticed that after a period of meditation you tend to hear, see, and taste things with more vividness and clarity than you do ordinarily. This common aftereffect of meditating is due to the change of awareness that comes during the meditation period. Our minds and thought process become much less dominant in awareness. The ordinary habit of desensitizing ourselves in order to think is broken in meditation periods, and the senses assert their perhaps natural place in awareness. In the exercises that follow for each sense, this process is made explicit, by focusing in meditation upon the senses and connecting each sense in turn with our center, so we see or hear or touch not with dulled senses but *through* the senses *with* our center. It becomes a process of each sense being opened so that we become aware at our center of what each sense beholds.

Listening Exercise. Assuming the sitting position of the centering exercise in your room, relax in open-eyed meditation, using the centering exercise for ten minutes. Play a tape or record of music that is without lyrics, such as a symphony or piano concerto. If you have access to one of the recordings of environmental sounds, which reproduce the sound of waves, wind, or birds, you may use it successfully as well. Avoid exciting music or music that includes the human voice.

Returning to the centering exercise, try to "hear" the music with your belly center, as if your whole body has become an ear. Do not try to listen with your little ears on your head, but listen with your whole awareness, relaxed, open, your awareness being played upon by the sound. As you fully listen with and from your center, your self-awareness as listener should diminish, and you will have the feeling that the music *is* you, that there is no separation between your space and the music's space. Continue sitting until the music ceases, then sit quietly listening to the silence.

After listening in this fashion in a controlled meditation environment a few times, you should be able to slip into listening from the center at any time in almost any place. Try listening to birds, to human footsteps, to your own breathing, with and from your center, as if these sounds are filling your center. Then progress to listening to human voices with your center, in which case you will discover dimensions of listening that we do not take into account when we listen only to the meaning of the words another speaks.

Seeing Exercise.   Assuming the sitting position of the centering exercise in your room, relax in open-eyed meditation, practicing the centering exercise of JUST SITTING for ten minutes. Place one favorite object, such as a cup, abstract painting, or other object without words on it, in a position three to six feet in front of you on the floor. Do not use a photograph or a picture of a landscape at first. You may use a lighted candle if the flicker of the flame does not make you drowsy. Returning to the centering position, first look at the object with your eyes, as if someone said, "Look at that!" After a minute, begin to cease looking at it with your eyes and begin to *see it through your eyes with your center.* This manner of seeing should feel very relaxed, with no eyestrain and with a looser focus than staring. If you normally wear glasses for seeing things at three to six feet, wear them during this exercise. Continue sitting for ten minutes, blinking your eyes rapidly if sight becomes blurred and letting your eyes roam around the object.

After seeing in this fashion in a controlled meditation environment a few times, you should be able to click into this manner of seeing readily under other circumstances and to practice the seeing exercise with moving objects and with human faces. The key phrase to trigger this way of seeing is "See with and from the center." By seeing in this relaxed and centered way, you will see details and aspects of things that are normally overlooked in your habitual way of looking and glancing at things. You will have the feeling that you are seeing things as if for the first time and seeing them more fully.

Touching Exercise. Assuming the sitting position of the centering exercise in your room, relax in open-eyed meditation, practicing the centering exercise of JUST SITTING for ten minutes. Then gently grasp two small stones with the tips of your fingers and thumb, one in each hand, with your hands in your lap and the backs of the fingers of each hand placed against the backs of the fingers of the other hand so the stones are held up by your fingers and your wrists are bent at right angles. Sit with open eyes in this manner for another ten minutes, spontaneously holding the stones still or rolling them in your finger tips. At first you will feel or touch the stones as if you are touching and manipulating them, that you are in control of touching. You will notice that after awhile you do not feel them, that you have become densensitized to touch. Now imagine, as you slowly revolve the stones, that the stones are moving through your fingers (rather than your fingers across the stones). If you cannot do this, move your finger tips across the stones as if your finger tips are examining the stones' surfaces. After moving across the surfaces, your finger tips cease moving and try to sense the inside core of each stone, one at a time, and then compare their cores. "Feel" the cores with your center, trying to diminish the habit of feeling that the stones are out there in your hands. Continue this process of "getting in touch" for ten minutes. This is not an easy exercise.

After practicing with stones in connection with the centering exercise, try to examine the surfaces and 'touch" the cores of other objects that you touch, hold, or grasp every day, such as pens, eating utensils, cups. Try to touch or grasp these objects with your center as well as with your hands and fingers. Also become aware of things that touch you, like a breeze, clothing, or the cushion you sit upon in the centering exercise. Finally, practice this open awareness of the center when touching or being touched by people.

Tasting and Smelling Exercise: Eating with Gusto. Since smelling and tasting are physiologically linked, the two senses are combined in this exercise, which can be practiced each time you eat. Combined with a plan to reduce food consumption for health purposes, eating with full awareness, by breaking old eating habits and providing more pleasure in eating, allows us to eat less and feel more satisfied.

As you sit for a meal, try to arrange yourself in a relaxed but alert sitting position. Before starting to eat, take a few quiet, deep breaths, focusing on your center with eyes closed. Open your eyes and inhale the aroma of the food before you. Try to identify the aromas of the different foods on your plate. Then proceed to slowly eat, making the process of picking up the food and placing it in your mouth a deliberate and gentle one that receives your fullest attention. Place the food in your mouth and try to taste and smell the food as you slowly chew it. Take smaller portions on your fork or spoon than normally. Do not overchew the food. Taste with all your awareness and focus on tasting. Taste with your center. After eating, sit quietly for a moment, focusing on your breathing. Keep relaxed and aware through the entire process.

If you are a smoker, try the same exercise with a cigarette. You will find that the taste and smell of matches and tobacco, to which you have become habituated, are rather unpleasant tastes and smells. You may also discover that inhaling and exhaling smoke is a poor substitute for the relaxing and refreshing breathing you do in meditation.

As a future meditator you will probably be eating three times a day like everyone else, but, unlike everyone else, you can make the routine of eating into an opportunity for meditation practice. Further, you will probably eat less and enjoy it more, again unlike many people who use food only habitually or mechanically as fuel for their bodies.

Interpersonal Meditation: From Competition to Harmony

America is a strange land. On the one hand, America claims to be a nation motivated by lofty moral ideals and directed by a vision of human purpose and action unique and superior. Many Americans trace their moral ideals and vision of human destiny to sources in the Judeo-Christian tradition. We have agreed to place the phrase "In

God We Trust" on American coins as a hopeful reminder of our basic orientation to life in this world. Yet ordinarily we are far from the attitude, sentiment, belief, and behavior proclaimed in that phrase. The coin is undoubtedly too often a symbol and means by which we reveal our absence of trust in God and Judeo-Christian values as the everyday and ultimate measures of our success in living. Coins and money are, in practice, the symbols and means of another method and measure of success. Deny it as we do with pious or wishful proclamations, money is a major measure of success for us, and vigorous competition against others (perhaps against our own inclinations), is an approved method of achieving success. So far, we must confess, we have been a people much more remarkable for our desire and ability to make money than for our willingness and capacity to trust God. A people who trust God will not desensitize themselves so they can more readily pillage the land and the world to acquire goods far in excess of their needs. A people who trust God will not tolerate, much less celebrate, a way of life that encourages distrust of neighbors, a frantic pursuit of material opulence, and an unending competition of many men and women against each other to reach the top of a ladder that leads to a nowhere of lonely pride and eminence.

The great and sad distance between traditional American values of trust in God, the inalienable dignity of each person, and cooperation to bring about the common good and general tranquility of all, on the one hand; and the everyday attitudes, values, and practices of trusting only in ourselves, using others as means to our private or limited goals, and pursuing a careless, narrow, and fearful life of struggle and competition, on the other hand, must be bridged by making the former, more noble values genuine and effective in everyday life. The time is at hand when we can see, more than in the past, the destructive, ignoble, fear-filled, and morally wrong consequences to ourselves and the land that follow from our desperate pride in self and our tragic loss of community and communion. We must turn around at the deepest levels of awareness and begin to practice new ways of trust in ourselves and in each other, new ways that cut across the grain of our old habits and create a new groove, a new channel of human fulfillment in community.

The meditation exercises of this unit offer experience and practice in a path to human interaction characterized by harmony, trust, and mutual support. Practicing these exercises, you should be able to glimpse the possibility and satisfactions of a way to interpersonal living that is free of fear, mistrust, and manipulation, and open to dignity, respect, and responsibility. The exercises should be viewed as practices of everyday use and value, and not as meditation exercises set apart from life. Through them you can confront your habits of competition, see their source, and, in this awareness, begin to overcome them. Through the exercises, moreover, you can begin to take effective steps on a different path of interpersonal living, a path more respectful, less manipulative, and more helpful to yourself and others than the path most of us follow out of habit, fear, social pressure, or immature values. Insofar as you choose to practice these exercises in your everyday life, to the degree that you make visible and real the attitude and commitment underlying them, you will have, in part, helped to create for yourself and others a new America as well as a new self. The spirit of human trust and harmony will be embodied in these exercises and put to work in everyday life.

These exercises are the final exercises and the perfection of the training program you have pursued. The exercises depend upon the preparation you have made in the preceding exercises. If your meditation is open to the environment, well-centered in your belly center, deep, relaxed, and confident; if you have been more successful than not in your daily exercises; and if your will-power has sustained you, you are ready for the leap into a meditation sensitive and helpful to people. Without the will power, work, insights, practices, and changes of the recent days and past weeks, you would be able to perform this group of exercises only in a superficial manner. In the future, your meditation practice will be sustained and completed only if you periodically return to the practice of the early, inward exercises and these later, open interpersonal exercises.

The following exercises are beginnings. You can and should go beyond them. With insight and good faith develop your own interpersonal practices, regulated by the best moral balance, guidance, and strength available to you. The purpose of these beginning exercises is that they simply and quickly reveal the roots of how we habitually relate with other people and point out a new way of being with and for others. Use them as a reference point for self-awareness and awareness of others, not as the specific and single *way* to further human harmony and trust. The way is long, difficult, and troubled. These exercises are merely doorways to the way; passing through them, we are headed in the right direction.

Hand Combat Exercise: The Sound of Four Hands Clapping

Most of us have gone through the motions of this exercise during childhood, approaching the activity as a mild competitive game. Standing facing each other, we would extend our arms forward and place our hands together so that one person's palms lay on top of the other's palms. The person with upraised palms would then seek to quickly pull his hands out from beneath the other's hands, swing them out and around, and slap them down on the backs of the other's hands before they could be pulled away. The second person tried to remove his hands from the path of attack. The game was won or lost depending on whether the hands were slapped or not slapped. This slapping game was a diverting activity, a test of nerve, alertness, and agility. Like many games, it was a limited, focused contest or competition, to be done in a spirit of play.

Like many games, the slapping game was a way of asserting and testing oneself against others, and a preparation for a competitive society. The worst players were those who refused to get in the spirit of the game by allowing their hands to be slapped again and again, as if in passive resignation, or those who, in the aggressive role, would wait and wait before striking. These players refused to enter into and submit to the spirit of the game: sharpening and testing oneself in a "harmless activity" whose essence was the will to compete with another, face-to-face and hand-to-hand, by "injuring" another or escaping "injury."

The hand combat exercise consists of using the motions of the game and transforming its purpose from establishing oneself as a victor or loser to discovering the source and process of our habitual desire to win or come out on top in relations with others. This desire is seldom visible to us as we go about planning our lives and living out encounters with others. The hand combat exercise brings the desire into self-awareness and makes us more conscious of its workings in other aspects of everyday life. The exercise also reveals that, at bottom, competition depends on a social contract or agreement to a view of life that there are winners and losers, that the game of life is to become a winner by discovering and attacking losers. The irony, of course, is that we have to agree, to harmonize our beliefs and actions, in order for this game of discord, of attack, of victory and defeat, to go on.

To practice the hand combat exercise, you should have no problem finding partner-competitors among friends and strangers. Play the game a few times as you would ordinarily, then proceed to the hand combat exercise, where the motions are the same but your attitude is different and your purpose is self-awareness, not victory. Before assuming the face-to-face, hand-to-hand "fighting stance," stand quietly and relax into your belly center, letting your breathing become deep. Focus on your breathing, letting your awareness rest on the rhythm of breathing in and out. Stand comfortably, feet at shoulder width, knees bent slightly, so that you feel physically balanced as well as mentally balanced at your center.

Proceed to play the game, remaining centered, calm, and self-aware for a period of perhaps three or four minutes for each round. It sometimes helps to arrange an elimination competition of several players in order to increase the rounds that you play and to provide an audience for each competitor's desire to win publicly.

If you are in the attacking position of hands on the bottom, observe the process by which the impulse to attack arises. Also, observe your physical, emotional, and mental reactions to a successful strike or an unsuccessful one. If others are watching, how does that affect your impulse to attack and your reactions to success and failure?

When you are in the defense position of hands on top, observe the process by which you become alert to the attack movement and then withdraw your hands. What are your reactions to your successful and unsuccessful retreats from the strikes of your opponent?

Where and who is the "you" that attacks, retreats, feels the flush of victory or the crush of defeat? Is this "you" the "you" you have relied upon as the source and basis of your meditation awareness?

After practicing hand combat exercises several times in self-observation, you should have a keen awareness of your competitive posture and how you mobilize your body, breathing, emotions, will-power, and mind to defeat the other. Does the same process of self-posturing occur in other, subtle encounters and interactions during the day? What feelings and thoughts arise when you consistently beat an opponent in the game? Do you change your approach and allow him to win some (even though this is cheating against the spirit of the game)? Do you change your approach in real-life games to allow losers to win occasionally? Why?

After competing with a particular opponent, one who is evenly matched, begin to lose deliberately and frequently, until you always miss your strike or always are slapped. If the opponent lets up, encourage him not to go easy. What happens?

This exercise is like a parable. You can see its meaning, as a way of becoming self-aware and of helping others to do so, in all daily encounters between people who are in tension and competition with each other. You will discover that we seem mostly at war with each other. You will also discover, perhaps, that it takes two to tangle.

Harmony Exercise: From Center to Center

The hand combat exercise brings into awareness our habits of encountering others in an aggressive or defensive spirit of competitiveness. It also reveals the cooperation that is necessary for the game of competitive encounter to be played. Can that cooperative basis be encouraged, made conscious, and practiced? The harmony exercise is an attempt to explore and practice the possibility that people can meet each other, more than they seem to habitually, without adopting the habitual postures of aggression or defensiveness and without attempting to be the victor or master over another. The harmony exercise asks us to practice being fully centered and open with others, to learn a disciplined way of living with and for others. From the insights, confidence, and centering gained through the harmony exercise, you should be able to gradually move into everyday encounters with others in a spirit and with a practical ability for interpersonal harmony, trust, support, and care.

Training in the harmony exercise requires that you have a partner who is a student of this training program or is someone with whom you can sit in confidence and trust, someone who is relaxed, gentle, open, and mature. If you cannot find someone to serve as your partner, you might practice the exercise with yourself in front of a mirror, give a copy of the training program to a friend who can become your partner later, or, neglecting the body postures, adapt the practices of centering and respond to opportunities presented in everyday life as you sit or talk face-to-face with people.

The harmony exercise progresses through several steps, from sitting back-to-back in meditation to sitting face-to-face and talking from your centers in meditation. The step-by-step progress represents a growth and testing of trust and comfort with each other.

The first step of the harmony exercise is to perform the centering exercise of JUST SITTING, but arranging cushions so that you are sitting back-to-back on the same cushion with your partner. Your lower spine areas should be lightly touching, but your upper backs and heads will not be touching if you are sitting properly with stomach muscles extended forward and a slight forward tilt to your torsos. Sit in this position for fifteen to twenty minute periods, learning to sense and adapt to the posture adjustments and breathing of your partner so that they are not disturbing. When you both are confident with each other in this position, move to the next step.

The second step of the exercise requires that the partners arrange cushions in order to sit in the centering exercise facing each other, with knees almost touching. Keeping your eyes open from the beginning of your sitting, gaze toward your partner's center, seeing the center with your center. Put all your energy into seeing with your center, not with your eyes. Sit focusing on CENTERING for fifteen to twenty minutes. At some point you and your partner may begin smiling or giggling because of the awkwardness or unfamiliarity of this exercise. Go ahead, but try to giggle or smile from your center; observe the impulse and process of smiling, how it arises, how it connects with your center, how it provides momentary relief and a defensive self-consciousness. When this is worked through, talk about it and go on to the next step in your next period of meditation.

The third step consists of sitting face-to-face and knee-to-knee, but gazing into the eyes of your partner gently, seeing with your center through your eyes. As you sit in this fashion, extend your hands to each other. The hands can be placed as they are in the hand combat game, with one partner's hands extended palms upward, forearms resting on the knees, and the other partner's hands resting, palms downward, on the hands of the first. The body and hand postures of this step express harmony and mutual trust and giving. What is expressed in body and hands can be felt if each partner sits well-centered and open to the other for ten minutes of silence.

The last step as you progress in the harmony exercise consists of sitting as in step three and then speaking and listening with your partner. Speaking and listening should be from the center, a way of communicating quite different in feeling and tone from our usual way of speaking and listening with our heads in terms of self-consciousness. What can be spoken of in this position? You might try chanting a mantra together or praying aloud. You might try an exchange of everyday phrases that we usually use to smooth relationships, like "Hello," "How are you?" "Good morning," or "Goodbye." "Goodbye" originally meant "God be with you," so you might try saying that from your center to the other's center. This is a good setting in which to share hopes, doubts, and disagreements with each other. The important key to this process of interpersonal communication is that both people throw themselves on their centers and trust in the center of the other, so they may be relaxed, alert, open, and responsive. There is a feeling of fullness in the moment and of authenticity in the words that will emerge during this interpersonal meditation exercise.

What you learn and practice in this controlled exercise can be a quaint experience or the beginning of an everyday practice, of seeking to be with and respond to others in many kinds of encounter so that you are open, self-confident, gentle, and centered with other people. People will be met fully by you and helped by your mastery of the habitual desire to be aggressive or defensive in interpersonal encounter and by your refusal to treat others as things, as useful, as role-players, as superiors or inferiors. Begin by practicing centering with friends, move to practicing it with people toward whom you are emotionally neutral, and complete the practice by centering yourself, your awareness, and your speech with and for those who excite emotions of great strength, those you love and those you hate. Soon you will discover the blessings to others and to yourself that flow from this way of being with and for others in depth and harmony. You will have discovered the discipline and freedom of loving.

Part Three

MEDITATION IN
EVERYDAY LIFE

Experimental Projects

You have now completed the training program of techniques, exercises, attitude changing, and awareness centering. No doubt you encountered problems of interruption, disturbance, and dryness, as well as insights and pleasures, as you moved through the days. If you are like most meditators, you found that certain exercises did not work all the time and that some of them did not work at any time. Nevertheless, if you have done your best, practiced regularly, and given each exercise a try, you now should possess an understanding and practical ability in meditation and have at your command several ways of doing meditation and of centering your awareness in differing situations, environments, and body postures.

You have now reached the stage of knowledge and mastery where you can knowingly reflect on the relationship between meditation practice and everyday life. Will you continue to practice meditation? How and to what degree shall your meditation practice enter into and possibly change your everyday activities and attitudes? Will you be able to find the time, energy, will, and meaning that are necessary to practice meditation as the months and years go by, as you and your circumstances change?

For most of us, meditation will become only a memory unless we practice regularly and with purpose. The best way to do this, some would say, is to pick up your roots and travel to a meditation environment and community. For most of us, however, the best way to meditate is to stay where we are and let meditation practice water the roots that we have. The best way is to find, by experiment, the exercises and opportunities for meditation and awareness that fit your life. Since meditation is a daily practice, the exercises you can best fit in are exercises done as part of your daily routine. If you walk every day, you can transform some of that walking into meditation walking. Your meals are opportunities for opening your senses. Your encounters with others can be transformed from habitual social or competitive games into meditation exercises in self-awareness and harmony. Friends and pets (even imaginary panthers) can become meditation partners. Once you see that meditation is not just another activity, but a disciplined attitude you practice in every activity, you have found the way to meditate in everyday life. And you have made the virtues of meditation effective for the lives of others.

It is to be expected that in the future there will be days,

weeks, and months when you will not meditate regularly and formally. You may, because of distraction, lack of practice, or illness, forget temporarily the feel or groove of meditation and of centering. Be patient with yourself. When you can, try to practice centering in a daily activity. When you can, try to practice the centering exercise. If you need to, repeat the training program of directed exercises. Remember that meditation is different in the life career of everyone, but once learned, it is always available as a resource that can be restored to full life by simply doing it with a will, regularly and patiently.

Turning Everyday Life into a Life of Meditation

The best way to pursue your practice of meditation in spite of obstacles is to join the practice of centering to an activity that you do each day. To complete this program of learning, you should now plan to devote one or two weeks to designing and carrying out an experimental meditation project, in which you take something you do every day, for a total of at least thirty minutes each day (such as taking three ten-minute walks each day), and approach it as a meditation exercise. For this first experiment, the activity should be something that you can do with skill and confidence already, such as walking or a sport in which you are competent and relaxed, and that takes at least ten minutes to do each time. Your self-designed project may be more elaborate than meditation walking or meditation in sports if the daily exercise is of a structure and rhythm similar to any of the exercises you practiced in the training program; for example, a project in centering while listening to or playing music might be an extension of environment meditation. All kinds of activities lend themselves to being transformed by a meditation spirit. Students of this training program have taken almost every imaginable daily activity and tried to discover the possibilities for practicing meditation as a way of performing the activity. Washing dishes, jogging, listening to recordings of the "Songs of the Humpback Whale," changing diapers, eating meals, taking baths, practicing karate, studying, greeting people, sewing, painting, writing poems, vacuuming the house, making tossed salads, dancing, singing, weeding the garden, playing pocket billiards, swimming, smiling—these and other activities have been found to be open to a meditation approach and to be available as the context of daily meditation practice.

Selecting one of your daily activities, write down how you will prepare for it or perform it as a meditation exercise. Give yourself a set of directions and begin to explore the activity and yourself by daily practicing, for example, meditation in washing the dishes. Keep an informal logbook if you like. As you go along, you will no doubt make changes in time and place, body postures, breathing patterns, and concentration devices. Aim at discovering the most relaxing, centered, and simple procedure for doing meditation in the activity. Carry through for a week or two weeks, perhaps writing your self-report down on paper as the conclusion of the experiment. I would welcome a copy of your project report if you wish to send one for possible sharing with others.

No better conclusion to this book can be offered than to present several project reports prepared by past students of the training program. The brief papers clearly articulate how the experimental project was defined, what happened as the meditation experiment progressed, and what conclusions were drawn, if any. Many of the papers include a final statement on meditation or on the training program in personal terms. The large majority of meditation projects are successful. A few papers detailing a failure in the estimation of the experimenters are included because they are informative failures. All papers represent only beginners' experiments.

At the end of your one- or two-week experimental project, stop all deliberate meditation exercises for a period of two weeks. This halt is necessary so that you can observe any tendency you might have developed to become narrowly habituated to meditation. Meditation should be a freeing discipline, not another habit. In this period you may also observe some changes in yourself that have come about because of the learning program. The two weeks will give you breathing space to assess those changes and to decide whether and how to continue your practice of meditation in the near future. Deciding to take up your practice once again, make it *your* practice, do the best you can, do not advertise yourself as a meditator, avoid getting "puffed up," and try to help others with the clarity, energy, balance, and strength that come with centered awareness. If you keep the fruits of meditation to yourself, they will rot; share them, and you will be fulfilled, a free and freeing friend of your city, of America, of the world.

This world of ours is wobbling, but ... *keep on centering!*

Meditation and Jogging, by L. L.

A family physician has told me that jogging proves to be an effective exercise for those who have mastered a daily routine of it, as it tones up body muscles, speeds up circulation, increases respiratory efficiency, and does a number of healthy things. I have also heard from various persons that jogging can be a good mental lift. I could never understand how I could achieve mental satisfaction—a calmness and lightness of the mind that people claimed—from jogging. One person told me that, by approaching the exercise in the right manner, she improved her total attitude toward life. Such claims made me wonder. This was before I became involved with meditation this year.

Last fall I kept a record of a jogging routine in which I described various physical improvements; not once could I produce an entry proving that jogging gave me peace of mind. So I began a *new* routine two weeks ago, the goal being to establish a more steady set of nerves and to "tone up" my mind! The first day of my new routine was essentially an observation of my former method of jogging and an attempted application of the newly desired method, that method being meditation. But the challenge of centering and maintaining serenity while simply walking somewhere, or sitting in my room, was not at all like the challenge that jogging while centering presented.

On that first day, while I bounced breathlessly in a sporadic way down cracked and uneven sidewalks, across busy streets filled with impatient persons in noisy vehicles, by yards full of barking, vicious-looking dogs, by construction workers who made all sorts of nerve-jolting noises with their machinery, and by a number of other unsatisfactory distractions, I wondered when and how I could ever reach a healthy state of mind balanced with a healthy physical condition. I could not even keep that thought in my mind, because at every second or third street block, some mischievous college man would proceed either to honk loudly at me or to shout a remark that was not exactly gracious. I actually wondered if I could achieve meditation with so many annoying distractions confronting me at once.

The next four days of the routine were basically the same as the first—experimentation with my awareness. I tried to maintain a steady jogging pattern, one that would not leave me so breathless after jogging only two blocks and up only a small incline. I also tried to find a way to put the big distractions under me *before* meditation; in the past I always seemed to be inferior to the distractions in their power to humiliate and frustrate me.

Once I achieved this heightening of myself and lowering of the undesired forces outside, on the fifth day, I jogged to the Stephens Lake area, which had fewer distractions, so I could attempt meditation more easily. Once I centered my mind into the lower center of my body, I began to join the pattern of my breathing with the pattern of bodily movement. I calmly counted inhalations and exhalations in accordance with the left and right movements of my legs, being careful to discard any attacks of frustration that might occur if the first attempt was void of success.

To my surprise, I found meditation while jogging to come naturally after about five to ten minutes of smooth centering. After awhile I left out counting and realized that, while I was gliding (instead of bouncing like an old ping-pong ball as before) over the course, the noises of traffic were not irritating me. This was a welcome sign!

The following days were filled with improvement in my body *and* my mind! I began to jog everywhere, not feeling too self-conscious to invade the university campus with my steady and revitalizing pattern of jogging.

At this point honking horns and rash remarks, or whatever the distractions, were still audible to me, but I gave them no real importance and little attention. The small amount of attention I gave to a honking horn was for my safety. I would then resume the rate of speed most effective. I am now still jogging for thirty minutes a day while meditating.

Meditation at first seemed impossible to achieve for me; to my satisfaction it began to be very attainable. It seemed like a crutch for a time, but then and now meditation is not *just* a crutch; it is *relief* for me, an accomplished satisfaction which seems to replenish my mind and consequently my body. I can now see the benefits jogging can have both mentally and physically, when application of the entire self is involved. This not only applies to jogging, it can apply to everything. The difference is great!

The Twinkle Toes Experiment, by T. J.

My meditation experiment was exactly that—an experiment. I did it for no important reason other than to satisfy my wild curiosity.

Objective: While in meditation, to walk through a darkened

room, by-passing obstacles placed on the floor. There is no use of any of the senses other than touch.

Experiment: My room is connected to a lounge. I started out in the lounge using sitting meditation. The lights were kept on in the lounge, so I would have night sight when entering my room. While meditating in the lounge, I concentrated on my toes, thinking of them as sensitive instruments—sensitive to objects, heat, and cold. I even thought of them as giving off light. After ten to twenty minutes of sitting meditation I would walk through the bathroom into the bedroom. My roommate had put obstacles in various places on the floor—anything from books to clothes. The obstacles were never in the same place twice.

Results: The first time I tried my experiment, I almost killed myself. I tripped over everything in the room, even things that were not meant to be obstacles. I ended up in my closet, on my head. I am not sure whether I was too excited or just not into the meditation enough. The second time I tried, I was more successful; I missed a stack of books and a pile of dirty clothes, but I ran into the bed. By this time, I began to think that maybe it was just luck that I missed the obstacles. Try again. This time I missed everything. What a thrill! My bruised body and I celebrated that night. I was sure it could be done now. The next night, I tried again. My twinkle toes led me around books, a birdcage, and my typewriter, and straight into a pile of silverware. I never realized until then just how dangerous and painful silverware can be. My roommate promised me she would never use silverware again (to my great relief). The fifth night was a complete failure. Just as I reached our room, our two parakeets decided to strike up a chorus. I do not blame them, however, for the wounds inflicted that night. I have decided that if I had been into meditation more, the birds would not have bothered me as much. The last night of my experiment was quite an experience. I missed all of the obstacles, but I tripped over the extension cord for the telephone. What a let-down!

Conclusion: For me, the experiment was a failure. I say this because of the fact that I was successful only one time. That time was pure luck, I believe. I am sure that meditation did help, because I am usually a klutz, but for me it was not a deciding factor. This does not rule out the possibility for others who are more experienced in meditation than I. I believe it is possible for one who is experienced. My concentration is not perfected enough for this type of experiment. Someday I might try again, but not too soon. I need time to recover. I do have something to show from my experiment—scabby knees and bruised elbows.

Meditation and Practicing the Violin, by N. K.

The practice of meditation has been very helpful to me, not only in preparing for a musical performance, but also in everyday activities. I have found that I can practice a type of informal meditation in activities such as walking from place to place, riding in a car, eating meals, and taking pictures of nature. In this type of informal meditation I become very aware of my breathing and my stomach expanding and contracting. I try to devote my attention to one particular thing while I am involved in the activity. This informal type of meditation relaxes me when I would normally be nervous.

The formal practice of meditation (sitting in lotus position) has also been very valuable to me. It has shown me that my self-discipline is probably not what it should be, as exemplified in a three-day period when I could not find time to meditate. The practice of meditation has also helped me develop a closer concentration to important events. I have been able to block out other thoughts and concentrate on one thing, devoting my entire strength and energy to it. Meditation has also made me more aware of how I treat my body—which things are good for it and which things harm it. I have been more conscious of the kinds of food I eat and how I feel after eating. Lately I have been trying to gear the amount of food to the types of activities

I am involved in. Because of this, I believe that I feel better physically now than I have in quite awhile. During the past year I had worried about quite a few things and had become a fairly nervous, hyperkinetic person. This summer, with the help of meditation instruction, I can relax when I need to, even though everything around me might be terribly busy and hectic. Also, I find that I am much more secure and happy when I am able to relax.

My special meditation project involved practicing the violin in preparation for a performance with an orchestra. The project began roughly on June 24 and ended on July 12, the night of the performance. In the past I have often become very nervous and tense before performing for special occasions, and I thought that meditation might help me to keep calm and relaxed under a lot of pressure.

This meditation project went through many modifications. I began with the thought of stabilizing or centering my body while I practiced. This involved relaxing my arms and shoulders and keeping everything flexible instead of tense, which I am inclined to do occasionally. After I felt at ease with myself and the position of the violin, I tried to find a stable position— one in which my feet and legs would give me good support. I worked on this type of exercise for three or four days and found that it helped somewhat.

The next step I went through was centering myself so that after I had found a stable position and felt fairly relaxed while playing, I would concentrate entirely on my fingers. I tried to concentrate almost entirely on the movement of my fingers and the type of sound produced. This, to me, was extremely difficult because it was so hard to key in on the fingers without letting other thoughts go through my mind. I worked on this part of the meditation and tried to perfect it all the way up to the concert performance date.

After focusing concentration and stabilizing my body, I began to meditate before practicing. This was a very positive experience for me. I really feel that meditating before playing can make you more alert. I also feel that after meditating energy is restored to the body. In these meditation sessions I tried many different exercises. The most positive results came after I meditated in the lotus position with my eyes closed. During these times I meditated on OM (a mantra) or the koan which was suggested to me, "Who is nervous? Where? When? Why?" or just simply followed my breathing while different thoughts filtered through my mind. Probably the koan was the most valuable to me because it helped me to put aside some of the insecurities, anxieties, and illogical nervous habits I have had relating to performing on stage. Another exercise I used before practicing was meditating on a candle flame. This was helpful to me for focusing my concentration entirely on one thing and transferring it to the finger movement on the violin. Meditation before practice was extremely beneficial to me.

After going through all these different steps, I decided it would be best to combine them all, keeping in mind while I played that I would be on the stage performing. So I began each practice session with meditation, then stabilizing, relaxing, and centering my body and focusing my total concentration on my fingers. This type of exercise really helped me during practice and dress rehearsals with the orchestra. Each time I practiced with the orchestra, we would have a short break before I played. During this time I tried to find a place to be alone, to meditate informally, watching my breathing in order to restore energy to my body. The first rehearsal went fairly well, but it was very difficult to adjust to being stopped and having the orchestra rehearse for awhile before continuing. The dress rehearsal before the concert went exceptionally well for me. I had to concentrate on my finger movement, but at the same time I had to be aware of the orchestra for different tempos and intonation. Everything I had been working so hard at paid off because my concentration was so intense and my relaxed composure came through. It was at this dress rehearsal that I felt I played the best, had the best concentration, and really enjoyed playing with the orchestra.

The day of the concert was fairly hectic for me, but I relaxed and meditated informally while I worked for eight hours. When I came home, I isolated myself and meditated before playing the concerto a few times. At the concert I played four pieces, as I am a section leader for the second violins. Then, at intermission, I secluded myself to do some deep breathing and practicing. When I went out on the stage I felt relaxed and composed. Although I had a few short memory slips during the performance, my concentration really helped me, and within a few measures I was playing the right part again. For the most part, I was not as happy with the concert as I was with the dress rehearsal, but I am glad that I had the meditation class to help me through a very pressured time. This was really my first public appearance, because I have never performed with an orchestra as a soloist or given a recital. I think meditation is a very valuable asset for many people, but especially for people in the performing arts.

Meditation and Smoking Cigarettes, by L. B.

For seven days I used meditation for the purpose of quitting my cigarette smoking habit. I began this project with the intention of relying not solely on my will power, but on my meditation.

I never really enjoyed smoking in the early morning, even though I often smoked then, and my whole meditation experiment relied on this. For seven days, every morning after I awakened I meditated, using a lit cigarette, sitting in the half-lotus position in a poorly ventilated but quiet room.

I would usually prop the cigarette up in an ashtray and place it on a small coffee table, where the erect cigarette was parallel to my face. Some days I would sit as close to the cigarette as possible and allow the cigarette smoke to get in my eyes, producing a very irritating effect on my eyes. Other days I would place the cigarette in the same position and concentrate only on the smell it produced by taking deep whiffs of the cigarette smoke. The poor ventilation in the room heightened the intensity of the smell, and thus the utter disgust I experienced while smelling the cigarette smoke.

A few times I took a couple of deep puffs from the cigarette, which was much stronger than the brand I usually smoke; this increased the displeasure I experienced while performing the test. I held the smoke in my lungs for as long as possible and then exhaled the smoke very slowly. The combination of the sronger brand unfiltered cigarette and smoking early in the morning, especially on an empty stomach, produced temporary nausea.

The results of the meditation experiment were beyond my expectations. After about two days of meditation I had no desire to smoke a cigarette in the morning. The thought of smoke sickened me. I did not smoke at all for four consecutive days, until I ceased meditating, after which I started back smoking.

Just because I started smoking again I do not feel as though the experiment failed me, because now I do not smoke in the early morning or in the early afternoon hours, and I have cut down considerably at all other times.

I think that if I continued the meditation, my goal of quitting altogether would be feasible, because I do not enjoy smoking as much as I did before. Certainly I could control my urges to smoke by meditating and using the stronger unfiltered cigarettes to train myself. This sensory meditation experiment could probably help me lose weight and accomplish a variety of other goals which I have set for myself. Through meditation, one can probably conquer any bad habit or cut down, at least, on anything undesirable. By using any other object in place of the cigarette, and making it distasteful, one could test the exercise.

Concerning my experience in meditating, I have ambivalent, but mostly positive feelings. I was never able to reach a state of enlightenment, yet I do think meditation has proven beneficial for me. Meditation allows me to relax myself and think more clearly. I am better able to look at myself more introspectively as a result of meditating. One of the greatest benefits I experienced is that when I feel exhausted, I can occasionally meditate and refresh myself. I feel somewhat rejuvenated and, consequently, I feel stimulated to do something constructive.

Gardening Meditation, by E. B. H.

I began this two-week project with the intention of meditating at least twenty minutes each day while I was hand weeding my garden. It was my thought that during this experiment I would feel in closer harmony with the life-force operating in the growth of my crops. I sought to center myself and become a balanced part of nature.

During the first three days I had set myself to the task of weeding most of my garden, which is about 100 by 75 feet. There had been lots of rain and through the golden hay mulch had sprouted most of my intentional seeds as well as a cover of local weeds. My days in the garden began soon after sunrise, and I worked the soil until the sun had set. My body felt good as the sun's rays gave me warmth and energy. As I weeded further, I was pleased at the size and health of the crops I was uncovering. They would now be able to reach freely for the sun, and the uprooted weeds lay as a mulch around them to keep in the moisture.

As I meditated, my mind continuously questioned my role as a woman in the natural process. I was playing the role of domination as I was intentionally selecting those plants which would live and flourish. I questioned my right as a single life to determine the survival of specific plant life. It disturbed me that I was uprooting plants that had also chosen my garden as their home. I do not eat meat, considering it an unnecessary, inhumane exploitation of animals, yet here I was, ruthlessly killing selected plants. Finally, I considered the folks who would share the food I had grown and realized that plant energy is the most efficient food source. I decided to leave those "weeds," such as lamb's quarter and nettle, which have nutritional properties.

The days that followed brought me intense joy, as I had satisfied my intellect and could concentrate on spiritual centering. The garden looked beautiful, and I could leisurely walk down the rows and pull the weeds I missed. There were no burdensome thoughts now to distract me, and the weeding was systematic enough to serve as a relaxing aid. At this point I began to experiment with various meditation techniques. Besides the walking meditation that I had previously been practicing, I also tried sitting in a space where I could easily reach around me. I would assume the half-lotus position and slowly and carefully uproot a plant and lay it as mulch. After I had pulled all I could reach, I folded my arms, closed my eyes, took a few deep breaths, and meditated for about twenty minutes. I was very calm and relaxed, yet alert and fresh when I opened my eyes again.

I also experimented with a longer meditation at the end of the day. I would face the western sky in half-lotus position and absorb the surrounding sounds: the whippoorwill, crickets, the rooster crowing, birds singing, trees swaying, and, alas, the tinkling of the wind chime. When I would open my eyes, I would behold the explosion of color as the sun disappeared under the horizon. I also found that I felt most comfortable in a special spot in the garden. It is deep within a large group of sunflowers, which are now about five feet tall and covered with large leaves. Being surrounded in such a way helped me to center myself and spiritually feel more in harmony and balance. It delights me to participate in this delicately defined process we term life.

> When the sun rises, I go to work,
> When the sun goes down, I take my rest,
> I dig the well from which I drink,
> I farm the soil that yields my food,
> I share creation, Kings can do no more.
>
> Chinese, 2500 B.C.

Meditation While Eating, by C. S. L.

The exercise chosen was meditation while eating. For a period of one week I was to find one meal per day, thirty minutes long, during which I could experiment with meditative eating.

During the week in which I experimented, I noticed one thing above all else: I did not seem to require as much food when meditating as when eating at other times. Truly concentrating on food and taking time with it could greatly improve my eating habits—and probably my figure. I have always been a person who "inhaled" food quickly, and in rather large amounts. I have noticed that if I talk with someone while eating, especially if it is an interesting subject, I cannot even remember eating. I seem to chew and talk at the same rate—hopefully not at the same time. Many times I am through eating a meal before the others have hardly started. One conclusion I have drawn from this exercise: I should avoid stimulating conversation at meal times.

Another troublesome area the exercise unveiled is the fact that I often read while eating. Much the same thing happens as when I am talking. I have finished the meal without realizing what I have eaten.

During the times I meditated while eating, I often felt as though something was missing from the meal. This was most noticeable the first couple of times. It was as though the table was not completely set or part of the meal was missing. I realized that the missing part was the conversation or the book. It was as if I could not remember the last time I had consumed a meal and really noticed the food.

Part of the problem with my eating habits is that I frequently do eat breakfast alone. And when I do, it has always been natural for me to read. I had always thought it was relaxing. But now I can see it is not particularly relaxing and is bad for the weight-conscious adult. I have learned a valuable lesson from this exercise: Know what you are eating and concentrate on the meal. It is much more fulfilling—in more ways than one.

One final thing I found interesting was the way my chewing, breathing, and thinking seemed to be in tune to one another after a few times. I became like a machine, but one that was capable of concentrating and thinking. I realized after a few times that, before the exercise, I must have really been tense and breathing quickly. During the exercise my breathing slowed and I was able to relax, a sure-fire way to ease indigestion.

I used a mantra a few times, but not always. I found one-syllable words or sounds were better while eating. One I tried was OM. Another one I tried to stimulate thinking about what I was doing was *food*.

I cannot really say I thought of any earth-shattering things while doing this exercise. I actually thought only of eating. What I did accomplish was new awareness of my eating habits, most of which I need to change. I found this to be a very constructive experience.

This training program was very good in showing the ways we can meditate in everyday life, even doing our most dull chores. I came away more confident in myself. I have really come to know *me*. Everyone can benefit from this, and I think everyone should find a meditation routine best suited for him. The most important thing to remember is that it is different for everyone. The program has shown how everyone can find a niche.

Doing the Dishes Meditation, by D. P.

The purpose of this experiment in meditation was to make a daily task more pleasant. Every day as I would stand at the sink and either wash and rinse the dishes or prepare them for the dishwasher, I would attempt to meditate. I tried this for about ten days.

At first there seemed to be too much noise and too many distractions. The very act of scraping and cleansing the dishes would get in the way of doing a counting meditation. When loading the dishwasher and trying to count, I would often put the dishes in wrong and would have to take out several pieces and try again. For a few days I gave up on that and just washed the dishes in the sink, rinsed them, and placed them in a drainer. It was easier to get centered, and after a few times a rhythm would develop. You can breathe slowly, count, wash, rinse, and set the dish down with little effort. While doing that, I could look out the window and observe summer flowers, neighbors on their patio, and people swimming. At the same time, my mind would be remembering a past experience or reminding me of some important date or to take some meat out of the freezer. I could be aware of the noises around me, people talking in another room, teenagers on the phone, TV news, baby sounds, and so on.

After this type of dishwashing became pleasant, I returned to the act of loading the dishwasher. I would take two deep breaths, get centered, and then scrape, rinse, and load. After a little bit of practice, I could walk about the kitchen and stay centered. I could return food to the icebox, clean the stove, collect soiled linen, and so on. If someone came into the room and talked to me, I would give them a nod-of-the-head answer and try to continue counting. My mind might wander off, and sometimes I remembered tasks or ideas I needed to remember and would take time to write them down.

From this experiment I gained at least two things. First, I learned to relax and enjoy something I had to do. Second, I became more efficient at what I had to do. I began to take more time with the dishes and did a better job. I became more organized and found myself planning ahead. It was fun to do the dishes and spend this time with myself. Now as I approach the kitchen sink, I just take two deep breaths and start counting "one ... two ... three...."

Meditation with a Hyperactive Boy, by E. H.

For my experimental project I chose the basic sitting meditation exercise. We sat cross-legged together in complete silence at his mother's home. We kept our eyes closed and counted from one to ten, counting one on each breath. When we reached ten, we would return to one. While we were counting, we concentrated on our centers. We meditated once a day for fifteen minutes.

B is a nine-year-old boy presently enrolled in the fourth grade. He is a hyperactive child. His doctor prescribes for him a stimulant called Ritalin, an amphetamine that affects the nervous system. B's blood pressure is high, which enables him to take this type of medication. The stimulant reacts in some way with his nervous system so that he slows down a bit rather than becoming more active.

B's mother is a truly loving and patient mother. She works during the day and is very active in the community. I got to know B and his mother through a baby-sitting advertisement I had posted. I baby-sit with B until his mother gets off work, four days a week, three hours a day, and Saturdays all day. I have sat with B since the fall and have enjoyed getting to know him and his mother.

I decided to ask B's mother if I could experiment with B and meditation. I asked her not to give him his medication on the days I sat with him so that I could teach him to meditate. She gave me her permission to experiment, but she knew his teachers would have a hard time with him on those days.

B's mother has always required him to nap one hour when I sit with him, so on the first day of the experiment I asked him if he was interested in learning how to nap without sleeping, although he would still have to be silent and keep his eyes closed. He was really interested in learning this secret. I told him I would show him how to nap without sleeping, but he must keep completely quiet until I opened my eyes. After B watched me meditate, I explained to him how to count along with his breathing and to concentrate on his stomach. He seemed to understand fully my explanation. We then tried to meditate together. The first day was the same as the three following visits—unsuccessful. It was obvious the lack of medication made B much more active. I tried to get B to sit with me, but all he could do was squirm. Although he sat with me for five minutes, he thought what I was doing was hysterical. He would open his eyes and watch me and get the biggest laugh out of it. Several times he would sneak out of the room when my eyes were closed.

On the fifth visit B was less active and generally more cooperative. We sat together for fifteen minutes, and when I opened my eyes, B was still meditating. I was really excited that he had progressed. What I thought was progression, however, was that B had fallen asleep. Even though B had fallen asleep, I feel it was an indication that he had relaxed. After an hour I woke him, and he was feeling very active.

With the next three visits I began feeling there might be some positive results. B was extremely cooperative. He sat with me and kept his eyes closed the entire time. He had not fallen asleep, which made me believe he was truly progressing and meditating. Although I truly felt B was meditating, his behavior did not change as a result. He was just as hyperactive before the session as he was after meditating.

My last two sessions with B were discouraging and proved unsuccessful. B was very active and uncooperative. He would not sit still and concentrate and would not even think of closing his eyes. It became very obvious that meditation was not slowing down B's behavior any. I feel B did learn to meditate and can meditate, but it was difficult for him to sit still long enough for it to be of any use.

I thoroughly enjoyed learning to meditate and the many techniques that apply. Being by nature a nervous and tense person, I have been helped by meditation in many different situations. Although meditation has helped me in these ways, it is something I do not feel I would carry out every day.

Meditation with a Friend, by M. L.

In the past seven weeks my idea of meditation has been radically changed. Before I took this training program I thought meditation was a way to put oneself in a trance, but I have learned that meditation is quite the opposite of a trance. Through the program, and my own experiences, I have learned that meditation is a way to become more aware, not only about yourself, but also about everything that surrounds you. I have also gained greater control over my body and, for the first time, I am able to relax myself and truly concentrate. I found that sincerely to concentrate on anything takes an incredible amount of will power; fortunately, I have been able to develop this. I feel this program has made me a stronger person and has increased my self-discipline.

I chose my project for a number of reasons. I found that meditating with another person whom I care a great deal about was an excellent way to communicate with her. I also enjoyed sharing the actual meditation, which I find very enjoyable, with a friend. The fact that we are friends and were able to talk openly about any problems that arose helped my project along.

My meditation experiment was carried out in two ways. The first part was done alone. I meditated by myself every morning, with my eyes open, trying to be aware but relaxed. As the week progressed, this became much easier for me to achieve. Noises, sudden movements, and other interruptions did not break my concentration. Things would register in my brain but would float right out again. This was a huge improvement, since earlier in the training program I was unable to hold my concentration if any type of disturbance occurred.

The second part of my project was with my friend. I feel that this was the most important part of the whole program. Every evening between five and five-thirty we would meditate together. We began by sitting with our backs to each other. The time spent in this position varied. We found that, if our day had been upsetting, it was helpful to remain back-to-back for longer periods, sometimes as long as twenty minutes. If we had had a nice day, or an exceedingly good one, we would sit for only five to ten minutes in that position. After we had finished sitting back-to-back, we would turn and face each other. Both of us would sit in the half-lotus position, with our legs touching slightly. We would place our hands one on top of the other. The feelings of giving and receiving changed according to whose hands were on the top. When my hands were resting on hers, I felt I was gaining strength from her. I would chant her name, and begin to feel as though we were fusing together. Instead of receiving, I was giving a part of me. I never felt as though I was giving back what she had given me; instead, I was giving her all the love and confidence I have for her.

At the beginning of the week we would grow restless with each other, and we would revert to slapping each other's hands. Unfortunately, that did not work, but we did find that smiling and grasping each other's hands calmed us down. Our grips would become looser as the tension slowly left us.

After the sitting was over, we talked about our experience. She sometimes felt impatient with me, that I was taking more than I was giving. That caused a few problems, but we talked it over and the meditation grew stronger because of it. She felt that the project went well but thought that if we alternated between morning and evening, it would have been more rewarding. Even though she enjoyed the exercise, she feels meditation is a personal thing and she would not do it with another person again. I think it was an excellent way to discover more about ourselves in relation to each other.

Our relationship was greatly strengthened by this project. We became much more aware of each other's feelings, and we seemed to develop a sixth sense about each other. I was able to read her facial expressions and her actions very well. We both learned to expect a certain type of behavior from each other in a given situation, and we began to read each other's moods.

I plan to continue with my meditation. It has become a part of my life which, at this time, I do not want to give up. I want to go deeper into it and experience some of the other aspects of meditation. I would never be willing to devote my whole life to it, but I feel it has helped me greatly.

It is a way of relaxing for me and a chance to become one with myself in this insane world. I have cleared my head of a lot of worthless thoughts and set my priorities straight. Unlike my friend, I would like to meditate with other people that I love. It is an important part of any relationship that cannot be achieved any other way. Meditation will make my life more pleasant from now on. I hope this has been a turning point in my life.

Appendix: A Five-Week Program

The training program in meditation consists of five units of exercises that progressively build upon each other in a set order and lead to a final, self-designed meditation project of one or two weeks duration. The five units of exercises can be learned, if not mastered, in a period as short as five weeks by beginning meditators who can arrange to meditate twice a day for twenty-minute periods. The following schedule is arranged so that each unit of meditation exercises is practiced for seven days. The schedule may also serve as a reference for meditators who cannot practice every day for five weeks but who wish to keep on a progressive and orderly path through the training program.

UNIT ONE: *The Fundamentals of Meditation: Relaxation and Concentration*

Day 1 Exercises
1. Basic relaxation exercise.
2. Basic relaxation exercise.

Day 2 Exercises
1. Basic relaxation exercise.
2. Basic sitting meditation exercise. Count *one* through *ten*, counting on both inhalations and exhalations of breath.

Day 3 Exercises
1. Basic sitting meditation exercise. Count *one* through *ten*, counting on both inhalations and exhalations of breath.
2. Basic sitting meditation exercise. Count *one* through *ten*, counting on both inhalations and exhalations of breath.

Day 4 Exercises
1. Basic relaxation exercise.
2. Basic sitting meditation exercise. Modify counting *one* through *ten* by counting only on the exhalation, while stomach is collapsing.

Day 5 Exercises
1. Basic sitting meditation exercise. Count *one* through *ten* on exhalations.
2. Basic sitting meditation exercise. Count *one* through *ten* on exhalations.

Day 6 Exercises
1. Basic relaxation exercise. Count *one* through *ten* on exhalations.

2. Basic sitting meditation exercise. Count *one* through *ten* on exhalations.

Day 7 Exercises

1. Basic sitting meditation exercise. Count *one* through *ten* on exhalations.
2. Basic relaxation exercise. Count *one* through *ten* on exhalations.

UNIT TWO: *Open-Eye Meditation: Centering and Walking Meditation*

Day 8 Exercises

1. Centering exercise. Begin with ten minutes of closed-eye practice, sitting on the floor on cushions in the half-lotus posture. After ten minutes, open your eyes. Count *one* through *ten* on exhalations throughout the session.
2. Centering exercise. Open your eyes after five minutes of sitting. Count *one* through *ten* on exhalations for the first ten minutes of this session, then focus on the word SITTING with each exhalation.

Day 9 Exercises

1. Centering exercise. Close your eyes until you feel relaxed and centered. Then open your eyes and focus on SITTING.
2. Centering exercise. Close your eyes until you feel relaxed and centered. Then open your eyes and focus on SITTING.

Day 10 Exercises

Today you should combine a centering exercise with your first walking meditation exercise. The combined exercise requires a thirty-minute period. Begin with twenty minutes of the centering exercise, focusing on SITTING. After twenty minutes slowly rise into the standing position described in the text. Walk a circuit for ten minutes, focusing on and walking from your belly center. Try to maintain the same sense of a center of relaxed awareness in walking as you have in sitting.

Day 11 Exercises

1. Centering exercise. Focus on SITTING IN AWARENESS.

2. Walking meditation exercise. Before walking stand in place about three minutes with eyes closed, focusing on your breathing, finding your physical center of balance. Walk for fifteen minutes.

Day 12 Exercises

1. Centering exercise. Focus on TOTAL SITTING.

2. Walking meditation exercise. Practice for fifteen minutes. Focus on WALKING; throw all your awareness into the swing and balance, the push and pull of just walking.

Day 13 Exercises

1. Centering exercise. Focus on ALL IS SITTING.

2. Walking meditation exercise. Practice for twenty minutes in three phases: walking meditation in the form of the panther walk (ten minutes); standing in meditation (two minutes); walking meditation, focusing on WALKING AWARENESS (eight minutes).

Day 14 Exercises

1. Basic relaxation exercise. Check for any tension, especially in the small of the back and in facial muscles. Close your eyes during this exercise, avoid falling asleep, and focus on RESTING IN THE QUIET.

2. Walking meditation exercise. Take a twenty-minute walk outdoors alone, letting your arms

swing freely, and focusing on WALKING. Keep alert to your environment as you move in it.

UNIT THREE: *Meditation with Words: From Silence to Prayer*

Day 15 Exercises

1. Centering exercise. Focus on the sensation of breathing in the stomach area.
2. Mantra exercise. Using the sound and word *one* as your mantra, inwardly intone *one* with each exhalation, letting the sound of *one* float from your mouth inward to your belly center, where each *one* will "layer the egg." Perform this exercise for ten minutes with eyes closed, followed by ten minutes with eyes open.

Day 16 Exercises

1. Mantra exercise. Using the sound and word OM as your mantra, perform the mantra exercise ten minutes with closed eyes, ten minutes with open eyes. OM is sounded like *Oooohmmmmmmmmm.*
2. Centering exercise. Focus on the sensation of breathing in the stomach area.

Day 17 Exercises

1. Centering exercise. Focus on the sensation of breathing in the stomach area.
2. Mantra exercise. Using the sound and word OM as your mantra, perform the mantra exercise. After ten minutes of layering the egg in your center with OM (eyes closed), open your eyes and let the egg contract and expand with your breathing. As you exhale, imagine that the egg is vibrating OM of itself, and that your body and mind are being "OMed" from your center.

Day 18 Exercises

1. Mantra exercise. Using OM as your mantra, lay-

er the egg for ten minutes with your eyes closed. Opening your eyes, let the egg vibrate OM on each exhalation, imagining that the "OMic" vibrations from your center are expanding like ripples or waves from your center out along the floor. End by sending waves of OM along the floor after about eight minutes and sit quietly for a few minutes focusing on your belly center.

2. Walking meditation exercise. If possible, do your fifteen-minute walking meditation outdoors. Let your arms swing freely. Focus on WALKING.

Day 19 Exercises

1. Basic relaxation exercise. Write down your list of koan questions as described in the text. Then perform the basic relaxation exercise, focusing on your exhalations and using the *one* through *ten* count as a focus.

2. Koan exercise. Using a key word from one of your underlined koans, meditate upon the word in the manner described in the text.

Day 20 Exercises

1. Koan exercise. Using the same key word used as your koan focus in the preceding exercise, perform the koan exercise.

2. Koan exercise. Meditate on the koan "Who is sitting and meditating?" The key word is *who*. Discover who *who* is.

Day 21 Exercises

1. Centering exercise. Focus on SITTING NOW.

2. Walking meditation exercise. If possible, do your fifteen-minute walking meditation outdoors. Let your arms swing freely and focus on WALKING.

UNIT FOUR: *Environmental Meditation: Opening the Senses*

Day 22 Exercises

1. Centering exercise. Focus on ONLY SITTING.
2. Thunder exercise. Focus on ONLY SITTING, in the centering exercise, as you play the recording of sounds described in the text, allowing yourself five to eight minutes of centering before the sounds begin.

Day 23 Exercises

1. Thunder exercise.
2. Thunder exercise.

Day 24 Exercises

1. Walking meditation exercise. If possible, do your fifteen-minute walking meditation outdoors. Let your arms swing freely. Focus on WALKING.
2. Listening exercise. Perform the centering exercise for ten minutes before beginning the recording of music. Sit silently for a minute or two after the music ends, continuing listening, but into the quiet.

Day 25 Exercises

1. Listening exercise. Perform the centering exercise for ten minutes. Using music different from that used in the preceding exercise, sit in the centering posture and center your awareness in the sounds of music. At the end of the music remain sitting quietly for one or two minutes.
2. Basic relaxation exercise. Focusing on DEEP RELAXATION, perform this exercise for fifteen minutes.

Day 26 Exercises

1. Seeing exercise. Perform the centering exercise

of ONLY SITTING for ten minutes. Place an appropriate object three to six feet in front of you and practice the seeing exercise for ten minutes. End by blinking your eyes rapidly.

2. Centering exercise. Focus on ONLY SITTING.

Day 27 Exercises

1. Touching exercise. Perform the centering exercise for ten minutes. Taking two small stones in your finger tips after ten minutes, practice the touching exercise for ten minutes.

2. Centering exercise. Focus on ONLY SITTING.

Day 28 Exercises

1. Tasting and smelling exercise. Perform this exercise at each of the three meals you eat in one day. Practice for three minutes at breakfast, six minutes at lunch, and as long as you can during supper. Try to avoid talking. If you are listening to others talk, listen as well as taste and smell from your center.

UNIT FIVE. *Interpersonal Meditation: From Competition to Harmony*

Day 29 Exercises

1. Centering exercise. Focus on ONLY SITTING.

2. Hand combat exercise. After playing the slapping game a few times to become familiar with the mechanics, play one or two rounds (three or four minutes a round) of the hand combat exercise while centered.

Day 30 Exercises

1. Hand combat exercise. Play at least three rounds of hand combat while centered.

2. Hand combat exercise. Play at least five rounds (fifteen–twenty minutes) of the exercise. Try to

remain centered, alert, and relaxed throughout the time period.

Day 31 Exercises

1. Centering exercise.
2. Walking meditation exercise. Take a meditation walk outdoors, if possible in the company of the partner who will practice the harmony exercise with you. During walking, focus on being physically balanced and awareness centered, and keep your senses open to the environment.

Day 32 Exercises

1. Harmony exercise. Practice the first step, sitting back-to-back and focusing on ONLY SITTING in the centering exercise.
2. Harmony exercise. If you are comfortable with the first step, proceed to the second step with your partner. Sit face-to-face, gazing lightly at the other's center and focusing on CENTERING.

Day 33 Exercises

1. Harmony exercise. If you are comfortable with the second step, proceed to the third step. Sit face-to-face, hands placed under or on your partner's palms, gazing lightly into the partner's eyes with your center. Remain relaxed and awake.
2. Harmony exercise. If you are comfortable with step three, proceed to the last step, speaking and listening, chanting, or praying. This session should last twenty minutes, including, perhaps, ten minutes for steps two and three before speaking in step four.

Day 34 Exercises

1. Harmony exercise. Practice step four, speaking and listening.
2. Walking meditation exercise. Take a meditation

walk with your partner, outdoors if possible. Speak together from your centers on what you are sensing, feeling, and thinking.

Day 35 Exercises

1. Centering exercise. Focus on ONLY SITTING.
2. Basic relaxation exercise. Let your mind review your experience in the training program. Focusing on those exercises that worked well, conceive ideas for your one- or two-week experimental project in meditation.

Notes

Chapter 1

1. For further study of the relation between the American cultural crisis and the appeal of Asian religions to some Americans, see Jacob Needleman, *The New Religions* (Garden City, N.Y.: Doubleday, 1970); and Charles Y. Glock and Robert Bellah, eds., *The New Religious Consciousness* (Berkeley: University of California Press, 1976).
2. For lists, descriptions, and addresses of hundreds of such centers, see Ira Friedlander, ed., *Year One Catalog: A Spiritual Directory for the New Age* (New York: Harper & Row, 1972.)
3. For more on the Transcendental Meditation movement by advocates of TM, see Maharishi Mahesh Yogi, *Transcendental Meditation* (New York: New American Library, 1975); Denise Denniston and Peter McWilliams, *The TM Book* (Los Angeles: Price/Stern/Sloan, 1975); and Martin Ebon, ed., *TM: How to Find Peace of Mind Through Meditation* (New York: New American Library, 1975). Ebon's book is an anthology of essays by different authors on subjects ranging from TM and Zen to biofeedback and the dangers of meditation.
4. An excellent discussion of the moral ambiguities of TM is in Una Kroll's generally favorable book on TM's psychological potential and relevance to Christians, *The Healing Potential of Transcendental Meditation* (Atlanta: John Knox Press, 1974), pp. 123–143.

5. Kurt Vonnegut, Jr. "Yes, We Have No Nirvanas," in *Wampeters, Foma and Granfalloons* (New York: Dell, 1976), p. 41.

Chapter 2

1. Two clear-headed and sympathetic analytical classifications of meditation approaches in different traditions are found in Claudio Naranjo and Robert Ornstein, *On the Psychology of Meditation* (New York: Viking Press, 1971); and Daniel Goleman, *The Varieties of Meditative Experience* (New York: E. P. Dutton, 1977).

Suggested Reading

The literature on meditation would fill a small library. The following books are but a small sample of what is available, usually in paperback. The intelligent meditator should be cautious about relying upon only one book or one author in interpreting meditation, so some of these books should be read to balance any bias of the author of *this* book. Other books are included because they are inspiring or delightful works on meditation, the meditation life, or the goals of religious meditation.

Benson, Herbert. *The Relaxation Response.* New York: William Morrow, 1975.
Benson, a Harvard researcher on the physiological effects of Transcendental Meditation, argues that underneath the TM technique is a basic psychological exercise for producing the "relaxation response." He proposes to teach people the technique for achieving the relaxation response without TM instruction and fees.

Blofeld, John. *Mantras: Sacred Words of Power.* New York: E. P. Dutton, 1977.
An authority on Buddhist contemplation, Blofeld records his personal experiences and interpretations of Hindu, Buddhist, and Taoist mantra, trying to place in perspective the lavish claims made about the miraculous powers of mantra sounds and formulas.

Brother Lawrence. *The Practice of the Presence of God.* Old Tappan, N.J.: Fleming H. Revell, 1958.

A series of brief and humble letters from a seventeenth-century Frenchman, conveying his efforts as a simple ex-soldier attached to a monastic order as he sought in simple chores the "presence of God."

French, R. M., translator. *The Way of a Pilgrim.* New York: Seabury Press, 1965.

The spiritual adventure of an anonymous nineteenth-century Russian pilgrim who sought through continuous prayer to become filled with the presence of Jesus. The book demonstrates how the "Jesus prayer" became active and central in the awareness and daily life of a dedicated person.

Goleman, Daniel. *The Varieties of Meditative Experience.* New York: E. P. Dutton, 1977.

Associate editor of *Psychology Today,* Goleman describes the Buddhist meditation approach of *visuddhimagga,* one of the most practical meditation exercises. Goleman also surveys with clarity the practice and interpretation of some eleven significant meditation traditions or schools now active in America.

Happold, F. C. *The Journey Inwards.* Atlanta: John Knox Press, 1975.

A brief introduction to the practice and meaning of Christian contemplative prayer, enriched by the author's knowledge and use of both classical Christian meditation and Asian meditation.

Johnston, William. *Silent Music: The Science of Meditation.* New York: Harper & Row, 1974.

Growing from the author's many years of teaching and research at Sophia University in Tokyo, the book usefully outlines scientific research into meditation, compares Christian and Asian meditation and mysticism, and links everything with the concepts of Teilhard de Chardin.

Kapleau, Philip. *The Three Pillars of Zen.* Boston: Beacon Press, 1965.

Director of the Zen Meditation Center in Rochester, New York, Kapleau compiles and comments on the lectures and theory of a modern Japanese Zen master, the late Yasutani-Roshi. Walking meditation and koans are discussed and described in the context of Zen life.

Lady Julian of Norwich. *Showings.* Translated by Edward Colledge and James Walsh. Ramsey, N.J.: Paulist Press, 1977.

Regarded by some as the greatest English mystic, Lady Julian eloquently wrote in the fifteenth century of her visionary experiences and of the love of God. This is a poetic, inspiring, and yet down-to-earth Christian approach to the life of awareness and prayer.

Lassalle, H. M. Enomiya. *Zen Meditation for Christians.* Translated by John C. Maraldo. LaSalle, Ill.: Open Court Publishers, 1974.

A student of Zen who has practiced under a Zen master for many years in Japan, Father Lassalle describes and compares Zen meditation and Christian contemplation, notes the parallels between Christian and Zen spiritual experience, and recommends zazen for Christians.

Merton, Thomas. *New Seeds of Contemplation*. New York: New Directions, 1961.

One of many books by Merton relevant and insightful for the student of meditation, *New Seeds* conveys Merton's personal experience as a monk with Christian contemplation. The framework is theological and Roman Catholic, yet it presents little difficulty for the non-Catholic wishing to include a Christian concept of God in meditative practices.

Reymond, Lizelle. *To Live Within*. Translated by Nancy Pearson and Stanley Spiegelberg. Baltimore: Penguin, 1971.

This sensitive, philosophical, and fascinating account by a Western woman living five years in the Himalayas as a student of a Hindu master reveals the master-student relationship so rare these days in the practice and learning of meditation. It also contains talks by her teacher, Shri Anirvan.